George Wither

Exercises Upon the First Psalme

Both in Prose and Verse

George Wither

Exercises Upon the First Psalme
Both in Prose and Verse

ISBN/EAN: 9783744687331

Printed in Europe, USA, Canada, Australia, Japan

Cover: Foto ©Thomas Meinert / pixelio.de

More available books at **www.hansebooks.com**

EXERCISES

VPON THE

FIRST PSALME.

Both in Profe and Verfe.

BY

GEORGE WITHER.

PRINTED FOR THE SPENSER SOCIETY.

1882.

Printed by Charles E. Simms,
Manchester.

EXERCISES
VPON THE
Firſt PSALME.

Both in Proſe and Verſe.

By GEO: WITHER,
Of the Societie of
Lincolnes Inne.

But, his delight is in the Law of the LORD. &c.
PSAL. I. verſ. 2.

LONDON,
Printed by *Edw. Griffin,* for *Iohn Harriſon,*
and are to be ſold at his ſhop, in *Pater*
Noſter Row, at the ſigne of the
Golden Vnicorne. 1620.

TO

THE NOBLE

YOVNG GENTLE-MAN,
S^r. I O H N S M I T H, Knight;
onely Sonne to the honourable
Knight, S^r. T H O M A S S M I T H,
Gouernour of the *Eaſt-India*
Company, &c. The Author
of theſe Exerciſes, *heartily*
wiſheth all true happi-
neſſe whatſoeuer.

S I R,

 Vch hath beene the re-
ſpect, and many the
courteſies ; which, I
haue receiued from your no-
ble Father. And the greateſt re-

A 3   quitall

quitall I can giue him; is, to make my felfe (as far as in mee lyeth) fuch a one, as that hee neede not repent, nor be afha-med of the refpect hee hath fhowne mee : and that, if I fhould dye vnable to repay his kindneffes ; he might yet, haue fome caufe, to think his fauors not altogether loft vpon mee. Nay rather, might reckon them among the good deedes he hath done) in regard I haue made vfe of them, (not to fol-low my pleafures, but) to ena-ble me in fome good endea-uours.

Of which, this little volume is a part; & knowing, I fhould well

well witneſſe my loue vnto
him, whenſoeuer I gaue good
teſtimony of mine honeſt affe-
ction towards you. Lo, as a
pledge therof, I conſecrate to
your vſe, theſe *Exerciſes*. And,
with your name, deliuer them
ouer to the world. That, when,
and wherefoeuer they ſhall be
read ; you may be remembred,
both for a louer of theſe kinds
of ſtudies, & a Fauourer of his,
who was deſirous to bee ho-
neſtly employed. For, ſuch
haue you approued your ſelfe
towards mee, both in your
courteous familiarity : and by
that free acceſſe, which in my
meditations, I haue alwayes
A 4   had

had to your Library.

Accept then theſe papers; &
let it not be tedious vnto you,
ſometime to read them ouer.
For, though I may be thought
fitter by many, to accompany
you in the way of pleaſures:
then to preſent you with any
found precepts of morality, or
Religion. Yet, I hope, you
ſhall finde me an Inſtrument:
readier to encourage you, in e-
uery of thoſe vertues, wherwith
your education hath acquain-
ted your youth: then to whi-
ſper ought, that may bring you
in loue with thoſe vanities;
whereunto, ouer-many other
of our Gentry, are ſo much en-
clinde.

clinde. For, though that way,
I might haue more bettered
my fortunes, and efteeme, a-
mong fome men. This way,
I am fure, I fhall better fatisfie
my confcience, and my dutie
to God.

Neuertheleffe, I prefer not
this to inftruct you; but, to
be a Remembrancer, of thofe
things, in which you haue al-
readie beene inftructed. For,
your good Father, hath not
onely largely prouided for
you, the temporall felicities :
but, afmuch, as in him lieth,
prepared you for that *Bleffed-
nes*, which is treated of in thefe
Exercifes. More he cannot do;
feeing,

ſeeing, it muſt be euerie mans particular endeauor, that ſhall purchaſe him this treaſure, being the moſt invaluable that can be For, the greateſt *Monarch* of the world, háth neither power to giue, nor take it, from you. Yea, and without it, the more of other bleſſings you poſſeſſe, the more miſerable they will make you. But, I know, you will bee happie in the proſecution therof, that you may treble that happines, in the poſſeſſion of it. And, to that end, you haue my prayers, who am

moſt faithfully yours,

G. W.

To the Reader.

*Know, that many of you, e're this time, expeƈted the firƒt Decade of the* Pƒalmes, *according to the promiƒe, in my* Preparation. *And therfore, when you behold here, but a tenth part of it, I ƒhall be thought to come too much ƒhort of what I intended. As indeed I doe (ƒeeing, I then wanted not much, of hauing finiƒhed the whole* Decade *in that manner, as I purpoƒed to ƒet it forth) But, if it were here fitting (or any way for your profit) to diƒcouer them,*

I might

To the Reader.

I might giue vndenyable reasons (to excuse my selfe) which I now conceale.

Onely thus much, I will say. Few men consider, how many painefull dayes (after the maine labour is ended) the writing ouer againe of such a volume will aske; how many moneths it may be afterwards attended at the Presse; how much charge, the Authors little means, may (without any profit of his labours) bee put to ; nor, through how many vnlooked-for troubles and businesses, hee must make way vnto the performance of it. For, if they did know, and weigh this ; so many, that are idle ones themselues, would not so often (as I heare they doe) blame my idlenesse.

To the Reader.

idleneſſe. But, rather wonder, how; and when, I got meanes and time, to performe what is already done.

Diſcouragements, and hinderances, I haue had many, ſince I began to meddle with the Pſalmes. *But helps, or encouragements, I haue had none; no, not the leaſt part of one: ſaue the comforts, which I haue found, within mine owne heart. And they are ſo great, that I am ſtill reſolued to proceed in this work, as I ſhal be enabled. For, though it may come the more ſlowly forward, by reaſon of ſome lets: yet, I am perſwaded, God will ſupply, by his grace, whatſoeuer, I am that way depriued of. And (if I can haue patience) bring what I intend, to much more happie perfeƈtion,*

To the Reader.

perfection, then if I had receiued no obstacle in the performance.

This Pfalme, *in the meane while, my friends were desirous of; and haue wished me thus to publish the rest, by one or two together, vntill a whole* Decade *be imprinted: That so (euery* Pfalme, *being an entire thing of it selfe) those poore men, who are desirous of them, and vnable to spare so much money together, as will buy a greater booke, may by little and little, without any hinderance furnish themselues of all. And beside, they thinke the portablenesse of it, may make it the more frequently read ; for which causes I haue hearkned vnto them.*

Take then in good part, this little beginning

To the Reader.

*beginning. Value it, as it shall de-
serue to bee esteemed ; And, let not
my vnworthinesse bee any blemish
vnto it. For, though I am no pro-
fest Diuine ; yet, my profession is
Christianitie, and these my labours,
hauing the approbation of Authority,
are not to be despisedly reckoned of,
as mine ; but receiued as the do-
ctrines of the* Church : *who hath
now, by her allowance, both made
them her owne, and deliuered them
ouer vnto you. So; Gods blessing on
you, and me, and farwell.*

G. W.

The ſeuerall Exerciſes

vpon this Pſalme,

are theſe.

1. A *Preamble:* wherein the *Author*, the *Perſon*, the *Matter*, the *Method*, the *Occaſion*, and *Vſe*, of this Pſalme, are treated of. pag. 1.

2. The *Metricall Tranſlation* of this Pſalme, with ſhort notes, to iuſtifie the queſtionable places in that *verſion*. pag. 9.

3. The *Seuerall Readings* of this Pſalme, in moſt of the ancient and moderne Interpreters. pag. 15.

4. An *Expoſition*, diuided according to the parts of the Pſalme: the firſt part begins, pag. 19. the ſecond, pag. 89.

5. *Meditations in verſe*, vpon the ſame Pſalme, beginning: pag 123.

6. A ſhort Paraphraſe in proſe, wherein the vvords of the Pſalme are vvholly preſerued. pag. 159.

7. A Prayer, taken out of the Pſalme, petitioning for the bleſſings; and to be deliuered from the vnhappineſſe therein mentioned. pag. 163.

EXER-

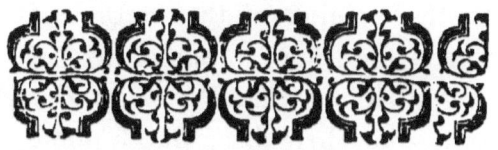

EXERCISES
VPON THE
firſt PSALME.

1. *Of the* Author *of the firſt Pſalme, and the perſon ſpeaking there: Of the* matter *alſo, and* method *of it: with the* occaſion, *and* vſe.

He firſt Pſalme (which hath no title in the *Hebrew)* moſt of the learned Fathers aſcribe to *Dauid;* as *Origen*, *Ambroſe*, *Baſil*, *Auguſtine*, *Caſsiodore*, &c. yea, and S. *Ierome* (though he elſewhere followeth

B

eth the opinion of the Hebrew Do-
ctors in his time) in one of his * Epi-
ftles, attributes this *Pfalme* to *Dauid.*
Some alfo there bee, who fuppofe it
to be compofed by *Efdras,* who is af-
firmed by *Athanafius* and *Hylarie,* to
haue gathered the *Pfalmes* into one
volume. But fince the Scriptures
make no certaine mention thereof,
vrging no man to follow this or that
opinion, I leaue it as indifferent ; al-
though I muft confeffe, that I my-
felfe am more enclined to their fide,
who impute this *Pfalme,* with all the
reft, to *Dauid.* But doubtles, whofe-
foeuer it were, or by whomfoeuer
the whole booke was thus ordered ;
this, was moft properly made a
Proeme to the reft, for that it treats
of *Bleffedneffe,* which is the principall
end of all Inftructions.

The *Perfon* principally fpeaking
in this *Pfalme,* is the *Holy Ghoft,* by
the mouth of the Prophet, who doth
hereby

* *In Epift. ad*
Paulin de om-
nibus facris
Scripturis.

The perfon
fpeaking in
the 1. Pfalme,
& the matters
handled in it.

hereby firſt teach vs who is truely happy, *verſ.* 1. 2. Secondly, by a Similitude, we are made to vnderſtand the excellent eſtate of him, that is ſo bleſſed. *verſ.* 3. And laſtly, wee are here informed, that the wicked being nothing ſo, dreame of a falſe vncertaine felicity, and are, both in reſpect of their preſent and future condition, moſt miſerable. *verſ.* 4. 5. 6. In breefe, this *Pſalme* may bee diuided into two parts, the firſt three verſes, ſet forth the bleſſedneſſe of the *Church* in *Chriſt*, and the other, declare the lamentable condition of all that ſeeke for happineſſe without him.

Something I will ſay, concerning the ground and occaſion of this *Pſalme*; for, I haue ſhown you before in my *Preparation*, that there were certaine diuine ſubiects, ſome of which the holy Prophet alwayes made the firſt *Obiects*, of his contem-

The occaſion of this Pſal.

Vide Prepar : to the Pſalter. cap. 5.

plations ; and the meanes, whereby he afcended vnto the cleere knowledge of the high Myfteries, deliuered in euery *Pfalme*. Now, although here be no *Title* to fhew vs fo manifeftly, what he made the foundation of his contemplation, that we fhould peremptorily conclude it, to be this, or that particular ; yet, by the matter of the *Pfalme*, we may (I hope) without iniury to the Holy Spirit, giue our meditations leaue to ayme therat. And to me it plainely appeareth to bee that Double-Law of God, which was giuen in *Paradife*. For, though at the beginning, God created man, that he fhould know, loue, enioy him, and bee made bleffed in that fruition ; yet, he would not that fuch bleffedneffe fhould be obtained without fome condition. And therfore hee gaue him an eafie, but (as I

Genef. 2.   fayd before) a Double-Law, partly affirmatiue, partly negatiue : the affirmatiue

firmatiue part was, that hee fhould
dreffe the garden, and eat freely of
euery tree therein : the negatiue was,
that he fhould not eat of the Tree of
knowledge of good and euill. And
there was both a promise of reward,
for his obedience ; and a commina-
tion of punifhment, if hee tranfgref-
fed : but *Adam*, who by obedience,
might haue beene eternally happy ;
by difobedience, was thruft out of
Paradife, into a world of miferies, to
wander for euer in difcontentment,
and in the vnhappy fhadowes of
death. Which God beholding with
pity, beftowed on him, in place of
originall rightcoufneffe which hee
loft ; a meanes of Iuftification : and
(changing the accidents, though not
the effence of his firft command)
gaue to him in his Word, that gene-
rall Law of Faith, by which hee, and
his pofterity, might bee directed out
of the way of perdition, and ariue

againe at true felicity. This Myfte-
ftery, being the firft in the holy book
of God, that moft neerely concernes
vs, the Prophet, as it feemeth, con-
templated, and made it the obieƈt
and ground-worke of this firft
Pfalme: For, as God gaue to our
firft *Parents* in *Paradife,* a negatiue
and affirmatiue Law, fo in that vni-
uerfall Law, impofed fince their fall,
fome things are commanded, and
fome forbidden to bee done; and
that Law, in refpeƈt of the effence, is
one throughout all the ages of the
Church. Moreouer, as *Adam,* if hee
had kept the Commandement of
God in *Paradife,* fhould haue there
liued a happy life, and peraduenture
beene tranflated from thence with-
out death, into a more glorious blef-
fedneffe in Heauen; fo wee, by kee-
ping the Law, which is fince giuen
vnto vs infteed of the Tree of life in
this world, fhall obtaine the bleffed-
neffe

neſſe of Grace in Gods Church for the preſent, and the perfection of all happineſſe (euen the life of eternall glory) hereafter. Contrariwiſe, as *Adam*, by contemning the Law of God, with the tree of life, in eating the forbidden fruit, loſt thereby the Eſtate of bleſſedneſſe, and incurred for the breach of a double Law, the danger of a double death ; ſo, thoſe which tranſgreſſe the two-fold Law of Faith and Workes, which he hath ſince giuen in his Word, doe both depriue themſelues of the fore-named felicity, and are the ſecond time (and that irrecouerably) in the way of eternall damnation.

The effect hereof is opened in this *Pſalme*; and therefore it may with good probability bee ſuppoſed, that he tooke the Parable, whereupon he compiled this *Hymne*, from the Myſtery of the Tree of *Life* planted in *Paradiſe*, and from the Law and

B 4   Charge

Charge which was there giuen vnto *Adam* ; and he fheweth, that as the tranfgreffion of the Commandement, is the way that perifheth ; fo the fulfilling of the *Law of the Lord*, is the onely meanes which is left vs, to recouer againe the happineffe that we haue loft.

The vfe of this Pfalme.

This *Pfalme* wee may fing, or meditate, when wee are difpofed to praife and fet forth the bleffed and vnfpotted life of our Redeemer ; or elfe, when wee are difcouraged with the profperity of wicked worldlings (which feemes to bee the onely happy men) we may hence, both informe our felues of their end : and comfort our foules, with remembrance of the bleffed eftate, of a good Chriftian.

THE

The metricall Tranſlation of
the firſt Pſalme.

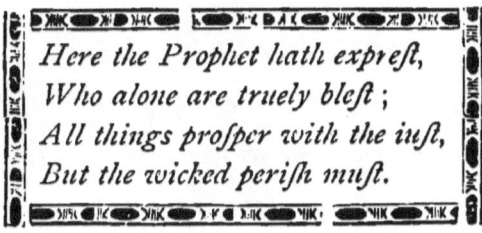

Here the Prophet hath expreſt,
Who alone are truely bleſt ;
All things proſper with the iuſt,
But the wicked periſh muſt.

T*He Man is* ᵃ*bleſt, who walketh not* ᵇaſtray
  In their ᶜlewd *Counſels, that ungodly are,*
Who neither ſtandeth in the ſinners way,
  Nor with the ſcornfull ſitteth in their chaire.

But, in the Law of the ᵈeternall L O R D,
  ᵉ Sincerely *placeth he, his whole delight,*
And in his Law, ᶠhis euer-bleſſed Word,
  Doth ᵍ *excerciſe himſelfe both day and night.*
                                          He,

He shall be like a tree, which close beside
  The [h] *Riuers set, his fruit doth timely giue* ;
His leafe shall neuer fade, [i] but fresh abide,
  [k] *And whatsoe're he takes in hand shall thriue.*

But with ungodly men it is not so :   (fann'd)
  For they are like the chaffe, which   ([l] being
By puffs of winde, is driuen to and fro.
  In Iudgement, therfore shall not sinners stand :

Nor the ungodly [n] (be admitted) *where,*
  The righteous shall [o] in one *asemble* [p] then :
For, [q] GOD *well knowes their way* y[t] *Righteous*
  But perish shall, y[f] *path of wicked men.* (are

---

[a] Bleffings, or all happy things, belong to that man, &c. For fome take the Hebrew word to be a Subftantiue plurall, and fome an Adie-ctiue plurall ; but which foeuer it be, it is fully e-nough expreffed in this our Englifh phrafe, *Bleft,* or, *Bleffed is the man.* [b] The word, *aftray,* feemes heere to be added onely for the verfe fake, but the fence indeede includeth it, feeing it is an erroneous

ous walking from God, which is meant in this place. ᶜ This Epithite is not added in the Originall, nor other, which I fomtime vſe in my metricall tranſlation of the Pſalmes : neuertheleſſe, I think I may, with a good conſcience, inſert them ; where they are either ſuch, as are warrantable in ſome other places of holy Scripture, to bee well vſed in that ſence : or ſuch as may bee naturally proper to the ſubiect, which they are applyed vnto. As I thinke this is. ᵈ This word, *Eternall*, is an attribute moſt proper to God, and indeede not to be applyed to any other. For, nothing can be rightly called *eternall*, but that which euer *is*, *was*, and *ſhall bee*, without beginning or ending : and therfore I haue added it to the word, L O R D, that it might the better expreſſe here, the Hebrew *Tetragrammaton*, יהוה ᵉ This, and many other ſuch like words, may ſeeme to bee added in diuers places of my tranſlation ; whereas, the power of the Hebrew being conſidered, they will bee found included in the Text. ᶠ Theſe words are added, *explicandi cauſâ*, and therefore put in a different character : which liberty, all Tranſlators haue taken, euen in their proſe-tranſlations ; and to authorize me heerein, I haue not onely the example of moderne Interpreters, but of the *Septuagint* alſo, who both *explicandi*, & *ornandi cauſâ*, haue added many words, in their tranſlation. As in the fourth verſe of this Pſalme, ὀυκ ὄντως, and in the ſecond verſe alſo, ἀπο' προσώπευ τῦς γῆς, neither of which, are in the Hebrew. ᵍ The word, *exerciſe*, which is vſed in ſome Engliſh Tranſlations, doth (in my opinion) better and more fully expreſſe the meaning of the Holy

Holy Ghoſt, then the word, *meditate*; ſeeing it may as properly bee applyed to the *heart* and *tongue*, as to the *hand* ; whereas the word, *medi-tate*, is neuer with vs vſed ſo largely, although it be ſometime ſo taken, with the *Latines*. ʰ *Riuers*, of it ſelf, aſwell expreſſeth the meaning of the Prophet in our tongue, as *Riuers of water* ; for, as by *Flames*, without other addition, we vnderſtand *Flames of fire :* ſo, without other addition alſo, by *Riuers*, we fully enough vnderſtand, *the water, diuiding it ſelfe into many ſtreames.* ⁱ Theſe words are *explicandi cauſa* alſo, as that, ſpoken of before in the ſecond verſe. ᵏ *And he ſhall make what e're he doth to thriue* ; ſo it may be read alſo ; for ſome tranſlate the words thus, *Et quicquid faciet, proſperare faciet.* ˡ *Explicandi cauſa*, as before. ᵐ In the firſt verſe, becauſe there are degrees of *Sinners* mentioned, and (in the Hebrew) diſtinguiſhed by three ſeuerall words, which the *Latines* interpret *Impij, Peccatores*, and *Deriſores*, that is, the *Vngodly, Sinners*, and *Scorners*, therefore in that, and in all ſuch places, where is meant more then one ſort of offenders, I haue called them, which the *Latines* terme *Impij*, the 𝕎𝕚𝕔𝕜𝕖𝕕, or 𝕌𝕟𝕘𝕠𝕕𝕝𝕪 ; and thoſe which they call *Peccatores*, I haue termed 𝕊𝕚𝕟𝕟𝕖𝕣𝕤 : but in this, and ſuch like places (where one kinde of euill doers is onely ſpoken of) I haue indifferently named them, ſometime the 𝕎𝕚𝕔𝕜𝕖𝕕, ſometime the 𝕌𝕟𝕘𝕠𝕕𝕝𝕪, ſometime 𝕊𝕚𝕟𝕟𝕖𝕣𝕤, and ſometime by ſuch other names, as I knew were vſuall in our tongue, to denote ſuch Sinners, as the Holy Ghoſt there poynted at ; for, howſoeuer the circumſtances doe in many places appropriate theſe words, the

                     𝕊𝕚𝕟𝕟𝕖𝕣𝕤,

ᵐ *The directi-on letter is heere left out in the verſe ; and therfore refer this note to the word,* Sinners, *in the laſt verſe of the fourth Stanza.*

𝕾𝖎𝖓𝖓𝖊𝖗𝖘, or the 𝖀𝖓𝖌𝖔𝖉𝖑𝖞, to particular degrees
of Offenders : yet in our tongue, we indifferently
vfe either of them, to fignifie the congregation of
reprobate-members of the Deuill. ⁿ Thefe
words are included in the fenfe, though not lite-
rally expreffed, *vide annotationes Francifc. Vatabl.*
º This is added, *explicandi caufa* ; for here feemes
to be meant, that great Affembly of the Faithfull,
which at the generall Iudgement, fhall bee per-
fectly made *one* in Chrift, who is the head of that
myfticall body. ᵖ I may feeme perhaps, to haue
inferted this word, *then*, more for the rimes
fake, then for any force it here hath ; but, being
well confidered, it will appeare to be neceffarily
added, for it hath refpect to the time of that iudg-
ment (fpoken of before) in which will be con-
gregated that principall Affembly of the righte-
ous, out of which all vnrepentent finners fhall be
vndoubtedly excluded. ᑫ I told you in my *Pre-
paration to the Pfalter,* that where foeuer in tran-
flating thefe Pfalmes, I met with the Hebrew *te-
tragrammaton* יהוה I would either expreffe
it by the word *LORD*, as the *Apoftle*, the *Sep-
tuagint*, the *Fathers*, and fome Englifh tranflators
haue done ; or elfe by fuch a word as fhould fome-
what effentially expreffe the Godhead : and diftin-
guifh it alfo by writing the fame in Capitall let-
ters ; as in this place, the word *GOD* is Cha-
ractered : Which (how euer fome may thinke)
is a fignificant, effentiall name of the Deitie ; yea,
(except the Hebrew *Tetragrammaton*, whofe
myfteries I am not able to fearch into) I thinke
there is no one word of any language, more fig-
nificant to expreffe the effence of the Deitie, then
is

is the word *G O D*, which though it be for diffe-
rence fake a little otherwife pronounced, is the
fame in fignification with the word of *G O O D*, an
Englifh *tetragrammaton* (out of whofe number and
forme of letters, if it were to any purpofe, I durft
vndertake to gather myfteries equall to many of
thofe which fome Iewifh Rabbines and Catalicti-
call Doctors haue framed out of the letters and
forme of the Hebrew *vnfpeakeable Name.*) It com-
prehends in it felfe all attributes whatfoeuer,
which are expreffed in the knowne Names of
God, vfed throughout euery language of the
world, for eternity, omnipotency, beautie, know-
ledge, loue, prouidence, bleffednes, with the per-
fection of thefe, and all other excellencies; ferue
but to make vp one *Summum Donum*, one Chiefe
good, and that is *G O D:* who, is the perfection
of all Goodneffe, and he, to whom onely this ef-
fentiall Name ought to be giuen. As appeareth in
Sᵗ *Matthews* Gofpell, Chap. 19. verf. 17. where
Chrift himfelfe telleth vs, that there is none to
whom this name of G O O D, appertaines, but
to the Deitie: *There is none good, but one*, fayth he,
euen God. And this is made fomewhat the plainer,
by confidering the englifh word, by which we
fignifie him that is Gods oppofite; for, we call him
not as other Nations doe, by a name comprehen-
ding fome one attribute of his, as the *deceiuer*, or fo;
but we impofe a name on him, which at once, ex-
preffeth all that can be faid of him in a thoufand
words, to wit, the *Deuill*; for, all the particular vn-
happineffes, mifchiefes, and wickedneffes of the
world, put together, doe make but one perfect
euill, and he in whom they meet is properly ter-
med

med the *Deuil* or *th'euill*, for it ſo ſeemes to haue
beene aunciently pronounced, vntill the Saxon
Character being ſomewhat like our D. made vs
looſe their pronunciation ; and as we call him that
is the fulneſſe of all Good, GOD; ſo; him that is
the protection of all euill, wee name the *Deuill.*
Theſe notes I haue added, to ſhew the Reader, that in
my tranſlation I tooke no vaine libertie, but made con-
ſcience of the leaſt variation, and paſſed ouer nothing,
vntill I had ſome reaſonable warrant for what I did.

Variæ Lectiones.

V*Er* 1. *Muſculus, & tranſlationes*
Anglicanæ reddiderunt in præ-
ſenti, *ſed Græcus, & Latina vulgata, &*
reliqui, tā veteres, quàm recentiories, le-
gunt in preterito ; *& alij habent* accedit
ad conſiliū, *alij* ambulauit in conſilia,
pretera Grec: vertit ἐπὶ καθεδρα λοιμοῦ.
i. in ſede Peſtilentiarū, *vt eſt, in vulg :*
lat: ſed Ieronim: habet, Cathedra deri-
ſorum, *ſic eſt etiam in recentioribus.*

Ver. 2. Deliciæ ipſius, *recentior:* vo-
luntas

luntas eius in lege domini, *vulgat:*
lat. In lege Iehovæ: *recentior:* in ſta-
tuto, *Chaldeus.* *Pluraliter* in ſtatutis,
Arabs: intelligens quæuis inſtituta Dei.
& vbi eſt, in lege eius meditabitur
in vulg: lat: tranſlatio Anglicana no-
uiſsima, & alij habent, Meditatur, *&*
Chaldeus, in luminatione eius cantat,
ſiue Iubilat.

Ver. 3. Et eſt velut, *&c. alij legunt,*
& fuit, *Græcus* κὶ ἐσται, *i.* & erit. Quæ
fructum ſuum dat: *recentior:* dabit
Genev: fructum ſuum concoquens,
ad maturitatem producens, *Chal-*
deus. Folium eius non marceſcit, *re-*
centior: non defluet, *Vulg. Lat.* &
omnia, quæcunque faciet, proſpera-
buntur, *Vulg. Lat. Chaldæus ſic reddi-*
dit, Omne germen quod germinat,
graueſcit, & proſperatur.

Ver. 4. Non ſic Impij *recentiores.*
Sic eſt etiam in Vulgat: Lat. & in Sep-
tuagint. ſed idem repetunt, vidt: οὐκ οὕτως
οἱ ἀσεβεῖς οὐκ οὕτως. Non ſic impij, non
ſic,

ſic, & *in fine verſus addunt,* ἀπὸ προ-
σώπου τῆς γῆς, à facie terræ. *Sic etiam
& Arabs.* Tanquam gluma *recenti :*
Puluis, *Vulgat. Lat. ſed idem ſignificat.
nos enim in occidentali parte Angliæ
vocamus tegumentum tritici,* 𝔇uſt.

Ver. 5. Non ſtabunt impij *recenti :
alij legunt,* Conſiſtent, *Græcus,* οὐκ ἀνα-
στήσοὺ], Nonreſurgunt. *Sic Vulgat. Lat.*
In iudicio, *recent :* in Die Iudicij
magni, *Chaldæus.* In fine, *Arabs : de-
notans extremum Iudicium, in fine
Mundi.* In Congregatione Iuſtorum
recenti. Alij in Cætu. *Alij* in Conci-
lio. *Græc :* οὐκ βουλῇ δικαίων. *Vulg : Lat :*
In Conſilio Iuſtorum.

*Nota, quod in libris Græcis & Lati-
nis, verſus tertius in duos diuiditur.*

The reaſon why I haue heere in-
ſerted theſe various Readings, and
in Latine, rather then in Engliſh, ap-
peares in the third chapter of my
Preparation to the Pſalter.

C   The

The firſt part of the
PSALME.

1. **B**Leſſed *is the man, that doth not walke in the counſell of the vngodly, nor ſtand in the way of ſinners, nor ſit in the ſeat of the ſcornfull.*

2. *But his delight is in the Law of the* LORD, *and in his Law doth he meditate, day and night.*

3. *And he ſhall bee like a tree planted by the riuers of waters, that will bring forth her fruit in ſeaſon, his leaſe ſhall not fade, and whatſoeuer he doth, ſhall proſper.*

The

The Expofition.

In nomine Patris, & Filij, &
Spiritus Sancti.

BLESSED: As a word of comfort, and a figne of good fpeede to my labours, ftands heere to make happy my beginning of this endeauor : and I humbly befeech the Euer-liuing God of *Dauid*, both to make *bleffed* my proceedings, & grant that my end may be crowned with the glorious reward, of eternall *Bleffednes.* For, that is the precious Iewell, which euer fince the world begun, hath beene the principall ayme, whereat euery man fhot, and the prize, after which they haue run. But indeede, the way it hath beene often miftaken, and among the *Philofophers*, which were accounted wifeft, it was a long time queftiona-

The way of Bleffedneffe, is by moft men miftaken.

C 2 ble

ble, both wherein this happineſſe conſiſted, and by what meanes it was to bee attained vnto. Nor in the times of heathen ignorance onely, were men deceiued in their aymes; but euen amongſt vs alſo, at this day, the greateſt part run wide, propoſing vnto themſelues, a happineſſe in the enioying of thoſe vaine things, wherby, they are often hurried quite beſide it. For, ſome place their felicity, or *Summum Bonum*, in hauing the ſoueraignty and authority ouer others; ſome, in abundance of riches; and the greateſt part, Epicure-like, in fleſhly delights and pleaſures, *Let vs eat and drinke* (ſay they) *for to morrow we ſhall die.* But the Kingdome of God is not meat and drinke, as the Apoſtle ſaith; and therfore that men might not ſtill bee deceiued, and ſo weary themſelues in a wrong courſe; the Author of this Pſalme hath here decided the matter in queſtion: and
ſhewes

In what things the Worldling placeth his happineſſe.

1 *Cor.* 15.

Rom. 14. 17.

ſhewes vs, that true *Bleſſedneſſe*, nci-
ther conſiſteth in obſeruation of the
mortall vertues, as *Philoſophers*
thought; nor in the worſhip of ma-
ny Gods, as the *Pagans* ſuppoſe; nor
in obſeruing the Law of *Moſes*, as the
Iewes dreame; nor in enioying the
pleaſures of this life, as great *Courti-
ers* and *Epicures* beleeue: But quite
ouerthrowing the opinions of all
theſe, and their fooliſh expectations,
who build their contentment on ho-
nour, riches, and ſuch like things of
this world; he affirmes, that man only
to be moſt truely bleſſed, and in the
path to higheſt happineſſe, who,
ſhunning the wayes of meere natu-
rall men, endeauoureth alſo to auoyd
the cuſtome of ſinners, to ſeperate
himſelfe from the ſcornfull enemies
of the truth, and to continue ſincere-
ly, embracing and rightly profeſſing
the doctrine of Gods word.　And
this kind of *Preface*, the Holy Ghoſt,

C 3　　　　　as

Why the Holy Ghoft vfed this preface.

as it feemes, hath vfed; becaufe, by difcouering (at the firft view) fo precious a Iewell, as *Bleffedneffe*; hee would allure men, to giue the more heede vnto thofe myfteries and inftructions, which are afterward deliuered: and, if it were poffible, make them more willingly conforme themfelues vnto the courfes, which are inclufiuely propounded. The like kind of beginning hath the heathen Philofopher, *Ariftotle*, vfed in his *Ethicks*; and which is more to be heeded, our Sauiour made it the *Exordium* of his Doctrine: as appeares in that his firft Sermon preached in the Mount, where he begins to pro-

Matth. 5. 3.

nounce, who are bleffed: *Bleffed* (faith he) *are the peace makers, Bleffed the poore in fpirit, Bleffed the meeke*, &c. and fo faith our Prophet. *Bleffed*, that is, according to the originall, *Bleffedneffe, Bleffings*, or all happy things, *appertaine vnto that man, who walketh*

not

not in the Counſell of the vngodly, nor ſtandeth in the way of ſinners, as it followeth in the Pſalme. And this his *Bleſſedneſſe* is double; for, he hath the hope and means of happineſſe in this world, and aſſurance of eternall glory in the next: or, as the Apoſtle expreſſeth it, *both the promiſe of this* 1 *Tim.* 4. 8. *life, and that which is to come.*

Now, what the bleſſings of this life are (which God hath ordained, for ſuch as walke in his ordinances) you may read in the laſt booke of *Moſes*; *Bleſſed,* ſayd he, *ſhalt thou be in Duct.* 28. 3. *the Citie, and bleſſed in the field; bleſſed ſhall be the fruit of thy body, the fruit of thy ground, the fruit of thy cattell, the encreaſe of thy kine, and the flocks of thy ſheep. Bleſſed ſhall bee thy basket, and thy ſtore; bleſſed ſhalt thou be when thou goeth out, and bleſſed when thou com-meſt in.* Yea, as it is in the ſame chapter, among many other temporall bleſſings, *God ſhall make thee holy vnto*

C 4   *himſelfe,*

himfelfe, if thou keepe his Commande-ments. Or if you would, in a word, receiue a glimpfe of the perfection of the blefsednefse, which belongs to the godly man. *S. Paul* giueth vs the beft knowledge of it, in fhewing how farre it is beyond the reach of our knowledge; for, faith he, *neither hath eye feene, nor eare heard, nor can it enter in the heart of man, what God hath prepared for them that loue him,* 1 Cor. 2. 9.

This *Pfalme,* as I fayd in the Argument, confifteth of two parts; in this firft part, is fet forth the blefsed eftate of the Iuft, and who is fuch an one: in the other part, the miferable condition of the wicked. In the two firft verfes, the *Blefsednefse,* and Piety of the man fo happy, is both negatiuely, and affirmatiuely defcribed; for, the *Prophet* hath begun, according to that faying of S. *Peter, Shun euill, and doe good:* and indeed, true righteouf-

1 *Cor.*

1 *Pet.* 3. 11.
Pfal. 34. 14.

righteouſneſſe conſiſteth, aſwell in eſchewing what may prouoke, or diſpleaſe God, as it is expreſſed in the firſt verſe; as in ſeriouſly performing, or endeauouring that which may pleaſe him (which is declared in the ſecond.) And, as a well experienced Phyſician, doth firſt purge away all the ill humours, that occaſioned the ſickneſſe of his weake Patient; before hee will adminiſter thoſe Cordials, which are prepared to recouer his health: So, by this order, in his deſcription of a bleſſed man, the Holy Ghoſt doth ſhew vs, that before the phyſick of his Word, can worke effectually in our hearts, for the ſaluation of our ſoules; wee muſt bee clenſed from the corruptions, which wee haue gotten by the euill-affected *counſells* of our owne hearts, or, the infectious ſociety of the wicked: and, as it were, diet our ſelues, by abſtaining from their abho-
minable

minable cuſtomes; which *Diet*, is here firſt preſcribed in the negatiue; And it is, as if hee had ſayd thus. *If you euer intend to recouer the health of your ſoules, and become partakers of true bleſſedneſſe; you muſt neither walk in the counſels of the vngodly, nor ſtand in the way of ſinners, nor ſit in the ſeat of the ſcornfull:* for theſe are the courſes which hee ſhuns, that doth arriue at *happineſſe*.

What manner of expreſſion the Holy Ghoſt vſeth.

But, the Holy Ghoſt hath not here vſed the ordinary manner of ſpeech, in his deſcription; but rather, by way of *Metaphor*, expreſt it: & the Diuine *Muſe*, hath into three *Traids*, or triple heads, diuided this *Negatiue*. In which are to bee conſidered three *ſubiects*, three *qualities*, three *actions*. And there is an admirable *gradation* in all the parts: firſt, in the *ſubiects*, or *perſons*; from an *vngodly man*, to a *ſinner*: from a *ſinner*, to a *ſcorner*. Next, in the *degrees* of ſinne; as, from the

the *counſell*, to the *way* : from the *way*, to the *ſeat*. Laſtly, in the *man-ner* of it ; from *walking*, to *ſtanding* ; from *ſtanding*, to *ſitting* : and their wickedneſſe, is increaſed to the full.

By the *vngodly*, ſuch are heere vn-derſtood, who are ſtill in their origi-nall corruptions ; and being ignorant of God, and his ſeruice, encline to thoſe euill affections, whereunto their nature is ſubiect. Yea, by the *vngod-ly*, are principally meant *Infidels* ; ſuch as are ignorant of religion, and the diuine worſhip of God, according to his Word : ſuch, as employ all their endeauours, without thought of him, to become happy in this life ; giuing themſelues ouer vnto coue-touſneſſe, pleaſures, with ſuch like vanities, whereunto their affections lead them.

The word *vngodly*, in our tongue, doth of it ſelfe, very well anſwer to this Explication ; for, as *Godlineſſe*

The firſt Triade. The vngodly, who they are.

moſt

moſt properly appertaincth to *God* and *Faith*; ſo, *vngodlineſſe* expreſſeth the contrary thereunto. The Originall importeth ſuch a crue, as are ſo reſtleſly affeƈted with worldly cares; and euill perturbations of the minde, that they are endleſly, hurried to and fro in their vngodlineſſe : like the ſea, which hath no power to ſtay it ſelfe. And ſo *Eſay* deſcribes them, *The vngodly* (ſaith hee) *are like the troubled ſea, when it cannot reſt; whoſe waters caſt vp mire and dirt.*

Iſa. 57. 20.

By *walking*, is Metaphorically vnderſtood, the ordinary proceeding of men in all their aƈtions, whether of faith or works. And in this place is ment, a *departure* from God in the progreſſe of their liues. And although in my *metricall* tranſlation, I haue expreſſed it by adding the word, *a-ſtray*; it is nothing from the naturall ſence of the verſe : ſeeing there is ment an, erronius *walking*, or wandering

Walking.

Pſal. 119. 1.
Gen. 5. 24.

2. *Chron.* 22-3.

ring from the right way ; as the word
abijt in the vulgar latine, verie well
manifeſteth : for, it ſignifieth moſt
properly, *to goe away.* And Saint *Au-
guſtine* ſaith, *Ille abijt, qui recefsit a
Deo.*

By *Councels* are here ment the in-
ternall deliberations of the minde ;
and that naturall inclination of man
to euill, which God ſpake of when
hee ſaid ; that the *Imaginations of the
thoughts of his heart, were onely euill
continually.* For, *Councell* is not here
ſo ſtrictly taken as *Ariſtotle* defines
it in his *Ethicks* ; where hee ſaith, that
*Councell is the finding out of the fitteſt
meanes to bring any thing to paſſe* ; but
Councell in this place, ſignifieth rather
Tempations, then ſuch Councell:
and it hath aſwell reſpect to the in-
ward perſwaſions of our owne luſts,
as to the outward aduiſe of others.
Euery man, ſaith Saint *Iames, is temp-
ted, when he is drawne away and enti-
ced*

Councell.

Gen. 6. 5.

Gen. 8. 21.

*Ariſt.*3.*Eth.*3.

Iam. 1. 4.

ced by *his owne corruption*, *Iam*. 1. 4.
But if you will know further, and
more particularly what the externall
Councels of the ungodly be, where-
to they tend, and what euents follow
them ; you may reade it in the *Pro-*
uerbs of *Solomon*, *Chap*. 1. *verf*. 10.
2. *Sam*. 19. 2. *Gen*. 37. *&c*.

Triade 2. Now, we come to the fecond *Tri-*
ade, in the Negatiue, which faith ; that
the *Bleffed* man, is fuch a one as doth
not *ftand in the way of finners*, and
here is expreffed a degree of wicked-
neffe beyond *walking in the Councels*
of the vngodly. For, by thofe that are
faid to *ftand* in the way of finners,
are fuch vnderftood ; who are not
onely led by the vaine deuifes, and
imaginations of their owne hearts
(which proceede from original guil-
tines) or fuch, who are fimply igno-
rant of God, and Religion (as the
heathen nations are) But, thofe are
thereby ment alfo, who haue fol-
low-

Sinners who they are.

lowed the *Councell* of their owne luſts, to put them in execution, with ſuch as are willingly ignorant of the worſhip of God; negligent of the meanes of their conuerſion : and offendors againſt the precepts of the firſt, and ſecond Table of the law. Theſe are ſaid to *ſtand*, not becauſe they walke no further in the path of vnrighteouſneſſe: but rather, becauſe they not returning back to the way of Godlineſſe, follow their wicked actions, with a ſetled delight in them : *Stant quia in peccato delectantur*, ſaith Saint *Auguſtine*; yea, they are ſuch as perſeuere vntill they haue gotten a habit in ſinne, and made (as it were) a beaten path in vnrighteouſneſſe. For, ſuch is the *Emphaſis* of the word, as it imports a *continuance* and *inſiſting* in euill : not a falling by infirmitie, as *Dauid*, and *Peter* fell; but a reiterating and heaping of ſinne vpon ſinne, through the whole courſe of their liues.

To ſtand, what it meanes.

What the
way is,
Pfal. 86. 11.
Acts. 18. 25.

liues.   For, the word *way*, both here,
and in other places of Scripture is
many times Metaphorically vfed
for Doctrine, or Religion ; and
fometimes for the manner of our
liuing, whether good or bad. But, the
way that the *Prophet* here meanes, is
that *broade and much troden way, lea-
ding to deftruction,* whereof our Sa-
uiour fpake, in the Gofpell of Saint
Matthew.

Ma. 7. 13.

And to make the matter more
plaine ; thofe that *ftand in the way of
Sinners,* are not fuch as vnwilling,
or through infirmity offend : For,
*there is no man on the earth that doth
good, and finneth not* (faith the Prea-
cher) but thofe who fetling there
loue vpon euill, haue gotten (as I
faid) a habit in finning : and fuffer
themfelues to bee carried headlong
by the concupifcence of their hearts
into all wicked actions, vntill they
haue by continuance made them-
felues

Eccles. 7. 22.

Who they are
that ftand in
the way of
Sinners.

felues not onely feruants to finne
and vncleanneffe : but euen blufh-
leffe, and without fhame, both of
what they doe ; or before whom, they
commit their follies.

Such, were the *Sodomites,* that pref-
fed into the houfe of *Lot* ; fuch fin-
ners, were the *Beniamites* of *Gibeah* ;
fuch, are all the keepers of publick
houfes of iniquity ; fuch, are thofe
common fwearers ; that when you
tell them of their oathes, will in
fport (to make an vnfauory ieaft)
fweare that they fwore not : fuch, are
they, that goe to bed late, and rife
early, to follow drunkenneffe ; fuch,
are thofe that fpend all their youth
in ridiculous vanities, and are diftin-
guifhed from the children of God,
by their language ; For, it often
foundeth *God damme me*; and fuch,
are thofe Gallants amongft vs, as
dare, impudently, boft of their beaft-
lineffe, or in merriment publifh their

Gen 19. 4.

Iud. 19. 22.

Eſay. 5. 11.

Pro. 23. 29.

D   owne

Gen. 13. 13.
Sam. 15. 18.
Math. 26. 45.
Luke 7. 37.
Iob. 9. 16.

owne lafciuioufneffe : euen thefe are fuch, as the holy-Ghoft meaneth in this *Triade*; and diftinguifheth from other offendors, by the name of *finners*; as appeareth through both *Teftaments*.

The 3. Triad.

What it is to fit in the feate of the fcornefull.

The laft part, or *Triade* of this Negatiue is : hee muft not *fit in the feate of the fcornefull* (that is) hee muft not haue fellowfhip with obftinate Hereticks ; nor carelefly, ftubbornly, or againft his owne knowledge, continue in vnrighteoufnes or vnbeleefe : nor fcoffe at Religion, with the profeffors thereof : nor infult ouer good men in their miferies : nor by blafphemous fpeeches, or erronious doctrines, malicioufly oppofe himfelfe againft God, and his truth : nor be affociated with fuch men, as are wholly giuen ouer to a reprobate fenfe. For, by *fcorners*, the holy

Scorners who they are.

Ghoft meanes thofe, who are not only guilty of originall vncleaneneffe ;

or

or polluted with actuall ſins ; but ſo
rooted in them, that they haue there,
ſet vp their reſt ; yea, they are ſuch
as, being hardned by their continu-
ance in ſinne, grow incorrigible, in-
credulous of Religion, contemners
of God, and ſo preſumptuous ; as
they dare reproach, blaſpheme him,
peruert his truth againſt their owne
knowledges ; and yet as it were in
deſpite of him, promiſe vnto them-
ſelues impunity : Such they are alſo,
as vngraciouſly deride the ordinance
of God ; and make Ieſts at his word.
And ſuch, Saint *Peter* ſaid, there
ſhould be in the laſt dayes ; euen *ſcof-*
fers, walking after their owne luſts, and
ſaying, where is the promiſe of his com-
ming : for, ſince the Fathers fell aſleepe,
all things continue as they were? Such
ſinners, and *ſcorners* as theſe ; were
the *Iewes* that deſpiſed *Chriſt* : Such,
are they that for temporall aduance-
ments, maintaine Doctrines againſt

D 2   the

Pet. 3. 3.

the knowne truth, and their owne Confciences; fuch, are thofe that make Religion a colour for their villany; *Deuouring widowes houfes, vnder the pretence of long prayer*: and thefe, if they once get into the *Chaire*, and fit there; are thofe finners which fhall neuer bee forgiuen: For, by the *Chayre*, or *feate*, is vnderftood; a defperat fecurity, and a diuelifh obftinacy in malicious wickcdneffe; and hee is properly faid to *fit* there, that continues in his peruerfeneffe, without repentance, vnto thc end of his life. And the reafon why there is no redemption for fuch, is; not becaufe there is want of mercy in God: but by reafon there is no repentance in man.

Thefe, make vp the three *degrees* of comparifon, and the third and laft ftep to the Diuell: For, to *walke* in the *councell* of the *vngodly* (which is the purpofe of finning) is bad: To
ftand

Mat. 23. 14.

The Chaire or feate of Scorners.

To *fit*; what it meanes.

ſtand in the *way* of *ſinners* *(*which is the action of it*)* is worſe; But to *ſit* in the *ſeate* of the *ſcornefull* *(*which is to die impenitent in his wickedneſſe*)* is worſt of all, and the higheſt degree of a Reprobate.

But, to draw into fewer words this expoſition of theſe three-folde Negatiues; by the *vngodly*, are ment *vnbleeuers*; by *ſinners*, thoſe that are vniuſt and diſhoneſt in their actions; by *ſcorners*, obſtinate Hereticks; by the *Councels of the vngodly*, are vnderſtood the vaine cogitations of meere naturall men, with the ſuperſtitions of *Iewes* and *Pagans*; the *way of ſinners*, is a vitious courſe of life, as the breach of the morrall precepts; and the *Chayre of Scorners*, is the obſtinate profeſſion of falſe Doctrines. Now, he that beleeues not the promiſe of the Goſpell, *walkes* in the *Councell* of the firſt; hee that adicts himſelfe to Pride, Couetouſ-

A briefe of what went before.

D 3   neſſe

nesse and such like; *stands* in the *way* of the second: And hee, that dies in the maintenance of a false worship, or in any of these sinnes, without repentance; is seated in the *seate* of the *scornefull.* Which the *Septuagint* calleth; the *Chaire of Pestilence.* And it very well expresseth the nature of that sinne: For, as the plague of Pestilence, is a disease most dangerous; infectious; and the suddaine deuourer of mightie congregations: So, those kind of sinners doe by their doctrines, contemptible speeches of God, and euill example; quickly infect, poyson, and kill the soules of an innumerable multitude of men. And therefore, obstinate Hereticks, Atheists, false Teachers, Scorners of the Truth, Deriders of Religion, and vnrepentent sinners; may very well be said to sit, in the *Chayre of Pestilence*: For, they are the plague of the world; and to be abhorred as a most

The Chaire of Pestilence.

moſt dangerous, and infeſtious Peſtilence, to the foule of Man.

And thus haue you this gradation opened; which may bee cyther vnderſtood according, to the ordinarie courſe : to wit, as from the poſitiue, to the ſuperlatiue : in this manner. He that is a bleſſed man, muſt bee carefull, that he *walke not in the Councell of the vngodly* ; much more that he *ſtand not in the way of ſinners* : but aboue all things, he muſt be moſt circumſpeſt, that he ſhunne ; *the infeſtious ſeate of Scorners*; Or, elſe it may be inuerted thus : The man that wold be bleſſed ; ought not only to auoide *the peſtilent ſeate of Scorners* & obſtinnate inrepentant ſinners : but eſchew alſo as farre asin him lies, *the aſtion, or iteration of any ſinne* ; nay, he ſhould not ſo much as ſuffer his thoughts willingly, to wander after *the vngodly perſwaſions of carnall deſires.*

The *Doſtrines* and *Obſeruations,*

D 4 to

The Doſtrines & Obſeruations ariſing out of this verſe. *Ob.* 1.

which may properly be gathered out of this verfe, are thefe. Firft, I obferue, that there be but three fteps to Hell, the *purpofe* of finne; the *aƈtion* of it; and an *obftinate continuance* therein, without repentance: and vnleffe we be very watchfull, we may flip downe thofe three ftayres, before we be aware: For, *Facilis defcenfus Auerni*; it is an eafy way to Hell: and the nature of finne is fuch; that it infinuates by degrees, into the heart, without being perceiued. Firft, it fcrues into good liking; and gaines the confent, or purpofe; then proceedes it vnto aƈtion. And fo forward, vntill it grow ripe; euen to the contempt of God: and this is the

The policy of the Diuell, to draw vs vnto the Counfels of the vngodly, and fo forth to deftruƈtion.

policy of the Diuell; to deceiue men: For hee knowes, if hee fhould perfwade at firft onfet, to renounce God: it is fo vnnaturall a finne; that it wold feem abhominable, to the worft difpofed men: & the hart would not admit

admit ſuch a perſwaſiō to take place.
Therefore, he makes not that appeare
to bee his ayme ; but preſents them,
rather with ſuch bayts, as ſeeme to
haue no danger in them. He counſels
them (according to the natural encli-
nation of their hearts, and the exam-
ple of worldlings) to ſeeke preſer-
ments, riches, pleaſures, with ſuch
like vanities ; hee ſhewes them the
glory and vſe they may haue ; he per-
ſwades the Chriſtian, who is in a
meane degree of life, that if he would
ſeeke after honours, he might there-
by become a Patron, for the afflicted
members of the Church, or Com-
mon-wealth. But he knowes well,
the olde ſaying will proue true, *Ho-*
nores mutent mores, Honours change
manners : and that preferment is a-
ble, not onely to make them forget
many good thoughts, and reſoluti-
ons, which they haue in a lower e-
ſtate : but to blot out of memory
alſo :

alſo, friendſhip, kinred, and the knowledge of themſelues (as wee daily ſee it doth) yea, the Deuill is ſure, that if hee can procure a man, but once to climb the ladder of promotion; it will ſo intangle him with the loue thereof, that it is twenty to one, but that he will renounce God, before hee will yeeld to ſtep one degree backe againe.

Others, hee tempts with eaſe; and makes them (poore ſoules) beleeue, that if they might disburthen themſelues of ſuch buſineſſes, or ſuch and ſuch cares, that they ſhould then better attend to the ſeruice of God, and with a more quiet minde, follow their deuotions. But the Deceiuer is ſubtill, and hath by experience ſeene, that afflictions make thoſe ſeek God, often and earneſtly, that being deliuered of their cares, cannot finde one houre in a month, to ſerue him.

Others, againe, hee allureth with the

the loue of riches: and that hee may
may do ſo, he cauſeth them to imagin
(perhaps) that if they were wealthy,
as ſome men are, whom they know:
there ſhould not ſo many poore
people, goe thinly clad; nor ſuch
numbers die, for want of ſuſtenance.
So many *Churches* ſhould not lie ru-
ined; nor ſo many works of *Pietie*, or
for the publike profit, bee vnperfor-
med. Yea, he perſwades them, that
theſe temporall things, may not only
be ſought after, and enioyed, with-
out the diſpleaſure, or diſhonour of
God; but ſerue him alſo for his ſer-
uice, and the better ſetting forth of
his glory. And indeed, ſo they may;
where they are moderately ſought
after, and gained by honeſt meanes.
But, where there is one that ſeekes
them, with ſuch temperance; there
are ten, who ſettle their mindes ſo
vpon them, as they choke up all
theſe good determinations, that
were

Few ſeeke the things of this world tempe-rately, as they ought.

were at firſt ſpringing in their hearts. For, a man that is not contented with his eſtate, but deſires things out of his owne concupiſcence, without re-ſpeſt vnto the will of God ; that man hath giuen the Deuill aduan-tage, and is *walking in the counſells of the vngodly* ; euen after the vaine co-gitations of an vnregenerate heart. And not conſidering the dangerous aduiſe, that his appetite giues him ; hee firſt ſuffers his thoughts, to bee buſied about thoſe vanities ; next, approoues of them ; and then ha-ſtens, to put them in execution : which aduantage, the Enemy of mans ſafety hauing gotten, hee cau-ſeth him to iterate, and augment his tranſgreſſion, vntill his heart growes hardned, and his conſcience loſe the fence and feeling of ſinne.

And ſo it comes to paſſe, that hee, who made no account of the tranſi-tory things of this life, and was tou-ched

ched with the guilt of ſuch, as the
world accounts moſt veniall ſinnes;
before he was allured vnto the *Coun-*
ſells of the vngodly : having *walked* a
little in them ; ſteps ſuddenly into the
way of ſinners. Which is a great broad
path, that leades downe a ſteepe hill,
vntill (without the great mercy of
God) he ariue at the *ſeat of the ſcorn-*
full, or the chaire of obſtinate impe-
nitency : and when hee is once ſo
low, and ſeated there ; the hill of re-
pentance prooues ſo ſteep, that hee
neuer returnes again ; but there con-
tinueth in a deſperate eſtate.

Hereby then wee are taught, that
if wee will bee preſerued from the
danger of ſinne, we muſt auoyd the
cuſtome of ſinne ; yea, the firſt en-
ticements, & leaſt occaſions thereof ;
and not preſume vpon our owne
ſtrength : for, hee that is content to
heare euill *counſell,* tempts God ; and
is not ſure, whether he will therefore
draw

Doĉt.

draw his grace from him, and fuffer
him to bee deluded by it. Concupi-
fcence; if it be not refifted, will turne
to action; action, to iteration; and
at laft, comes hardneffe of heart:
for, he that feeles in himfelfe, the euill
motions of luft, and can hardly re-
ftraine them, hauing no obiects to
entice him; how much leffe, will he
bee able to curb them, if hee come,
where hee may haue the beauty, and
wantonneffe of another, to inflame
him? Or, if he could not bridle his
affections before he had committed
vncleanneffe, when hee had more
grace, more fhame, more denials, and
many more ftops, to hold him backe,
from wickedneffe: Alas! why fhould
any man thinke it poffible, for him to
forfake it, at his owne pleafure, when
hee hath put himfelfe out of the way
of vertue; and hath neither inward
grace, nor outward meanes, to pre-
uent it? If, when thou hadft two
cyes,

eyes, thou couldſt not keep the way, being in it: canſt thou hope, hauing neuer an eye left thee; to find it, when thou art out of it? No doubtleſſe, if wee cannot keepe the ſea from ouer-flowing vs, when the bankes are whole; ſurely, after they are once broken, the breach will encreaſe, and the flouds will come in, vntill they haue quite ouer-whelmed vs: vnleſſe the mercifull hand of a greater pow-er, then our owne, help to recouer vs. A little water will extinguiſh a cole; but a flame is not ſo eaſily quenched. And therefore, we ought to kill theſe Cockatrices in the egge, and bee wa-ry, not to giue the leaſt advantage, vnto the infirmities of euill. We haue examples enough to warne vs. *Da-uid* was a good, and an extraordina-ry man; yet, giuing his eyes too much liberty, the euill *counſells* of vn-godly affections, got by thoſe win-dowes, into his heart, and drew him

on

on in their *walke*, vntill they brought him to the *way of finners* ; where hee *ftood* a long time, heaping one offence vpon another : And had not God fent a *Prophet* of purpofe, to call him out of that *way* ; as holy a man as he was, he had neuer of himfelfe returned, vntill he had taken vp his *feat with the fcorners.* And yet, for all this, wee, euen wee weaklings, dare giue our felues any liberty. We can willingly runne thither, where wee know before, that we fhall here fee ; nay, bee compelled, to bee partakers of finne : and notwithftanding, warrant our owne fafeties.

Some, I haue heard fay ; that in all companies, they could beare themfelues temperately, and among Drunkards, efcape free, though all their companie failed of that gouernment : but alas, they fee not their owne deformities ; for, I haue knowne, that fome of them, were euen

The bold prefumption of man.

uen then diſtempered, when they ſayd ſo.

Others, I haue heard, ſo confident in their owne vertues ; that they haue profeſſed themſelues able, to reſiſt the ſtrongeſt temptations of incontinency : and that, though they were all alone, with the moſt tempting beauty, and where they had the greateſt prouocations to folly ; they could neuertheleſſe keep themſeues, from any diſhoneſt act. This I haue heard: and beleeue me; I think ſuch a thing poſſible, if they rely more on Gods grace, then their owne abilities ; and came into this temptation, by accident, without wilfull ſeeking, or deſiring any ſuch occaſion. Yea, many (no doubt) haue eſcaped ſuch trials. But, if any man depend vpon his owne chaſtity, and purpoſely tempt himſelfe with opportunities, to doe euill ; hee, walkes *the way* which God approoues not: and therefore it ſhall

E   periſh.

perifh ; yea, although hee intended, at the firft, no more, but to haue it in his power, to doe euill ; it is a thoufand to one, if God giue him not o-uer, to be vanquifhed by that finne, which hee foolifhly prefumed to o-uercome.

Genef. 39.

Whilft *Iofeph* was about his bufineffe, the allurements of his Miftres had no power ouer him : and fo, whilft with him, we feek well to employ our felues ; though *counfels of vngodlines*, be rounded in our eares ; and ftrange vnlooked for temptations, with faire opportunities, lay fiege againft vs ; yet they fhall not preuaile ; no, not thefe that feeme Miftreffes ouer our affeſtions, and powerfull enough to command vs. But, if we leaue to be honeftly bufied, and, as many of vs young men doe, being idle our felues, feeke out thofe, who are euery way as idle ; and with vaine difcourfe, or vnfeemly geftures, paffe

paſſe away our precious houres.
Queſtionleſſe, ſomtime or other, we
ſhall bee betrayed to commit that,
which wee little thought perhaps, to
haue beene guilty of; and grow, after
a while, ſo baſe, to ſeeke that thing of
the *Mayd*, which wee preſumed the
Miſtreſſe could neither haue com-
manded, not wooed vs vnto. Nay, I
am perſwaded ; that *Ioſeph*, who hath
gotten the title of Chaſte : if hee
would haue left his affaires, and ven-
tured himſelfe, as ſome of vs doe, in
effeminate court-ſhips ; it is to be fea-
red, that the Spirit of God would
haue left him, as it forſook *Sampſon*,
or *Dauid.* And then, a meaner wo-
man then his *Miſtreſſe*, might haue
wrought him to her will ; and it is a
queſtion, whether he would not haue
proued the Attempter, of hers, or
ſome others Chaſtity.

The ſecond obſeruation, that wee
may take from hence, is this ; that if   *Obſer.* 2.

E 2   there

there bee degrees in ſinne, and ſeue-
rall ſteps, that lead vs from the way
of bleſſedneſſe ; we muſt not thinke
it enough, if we can auoyd ſome one
degree of ſinne. Nay, it is not ſuffi-
cient, if we ſhun all but one : for, he
that hath gone but one ſtep backe
from the right way ; if hee doe not
come backe that one ſtep, he is neuer
likely to ariue at happineſſe, though
hee neuer goe further on in a wrong
path. But it is impoſſible, to ſtay vp-
on any one degree of ſinning (with-
out repentance) and not to ſtep into
another : as appeareth in the former
obſeruation.

Obſer. 3.

Thirdly, if wee muſt bee wary, to
auoyd the *Counſels of the vngodly,*
& the impiety of misbeliefe ; aſwel as
to ſhun *the way of ſinners:* which (as I
ſayd before) is the committing of a-
ctuall ſinnes. Then, two ſorts of men
are hereby warned, to amend them-
ſelues, if they euer will intend to bee
bleſſed :

Two ſorts of
men, heee
warned to re-
pent.

bleſſed: The firſt, are thoſe morall
men, that thinke it ſufficient, ſo they
can bee counted iuſt pay-maſters,
quiet neighbours, honeſt plaine-dea-
lers, and ſuch as doe no men hurt;
though they neuer know what be-
longs to God, or Religion. The o-
ther, are ſuch Profeſſors, as ſuppoſe;
that if they haue heard Diuine Ser-
uice, twice euery Saboth; ſix Le-
ctures in a week; and ſlubbered ouer
their ordinary deuotions: it is no
matter, how diſhoneſtly they liue;
how vncharitable, and contentious
they be among their neighbours; nor
how irregular they bee in the courſe
of their liues. But, both theſe ought
to know, that God promiſeth not a-
ny *Bleſſedneſſe* to ſuch Triflers, as do
his ſeruice by halues; but vnto them,
that hauing both *religion*, and *honeſty*;
faith, and *workes*; neither *walke in the
Counſels of the vngodly: nor ſtand in
the way of ſinners.* For, all others are

E 3   in

in danger, to take vp their *feat* with the *fcornfull.*

Verfe 2.

Thus much, of the *Bleffed* mans defcription, by the *Negatiue*, contained in the firft verfe of this *Pfalme.* On which I wil enlarge my obferuations no further ; but come to the *Affirmatiue*, contained in thefe words. *But his delight, is in the Law of the* L O R D *, and in his Law, doth hee meditate day and nigh.*

Three things obferuable in the fecond verfe.

In which *Affirmatiue*, there are three things to bee obferued, by the bleffed man ; & they are oppofed to thofe three, which are to be auoyded in the former verfe : To the *walking in the Counfells of the vngodly*, is oppofed, *a delight in the Law of the* L O R D *:* to *ftanding in the way of finners*, is oppofed, *the meditation of the Diuine Word*: and, to *fitting in the feat of the fcornfull*, a continuall *perfeuerance, both day and night, in the true feruice of God.* Yea, thefe words haue

in

in them, an excellent *Antitheſis*, or contradiction, to the courſes of the wicked; who, employeth al his counſels, endeauours, and actions, in ſeeking vaine ends, and aduancing his owne wayes: while the iuſt man, ſetting at nought, all earthly affaires and delights, in reſpect of Gods will; is heartily in loue with his Word, and continually exerciſing himſelfe, in the ſerious meditating, teaching, and practice therof. For, the word *Ieghe*, which is interpreted to, *meditate*, hath reference, aſwell to the words and workes, as to the thoughts (in which fence, it is not vſed in the Scriptures only; but the Poet alſo ſaith,—*Meditabor arundine Muſam.*) And it was well expreſſed in the word, *Exerciſe*, in our olde Engliſh Tranſlation.

By the *Law*, is vnderſtood, not onely the morall Lawes; for then, *Bleſſedneſſe* might haue been obtai-

E 4　　　　　　ned,

To meditate, what it means

Pſal. 35. 28.
Pſal. 36. 30.

What is ſignified by the Law.

ned, by working, according to the morall vertues, as the heathen *Philo-fophers* taught. Nor, is here meant the Ceremoniall Law alone ; nor that, and the morall together onely. For then, the wicked *Iewes*, though they continued in their vnbeleefe, might become partakers of this hap-pineffe. But the *Law*, in this place (as I told you in my *Preparation to the Pfalter*, it was fometime to be vnder-ftood) fignifies the Law of God, as it hath at once, refpect to all the ages of the Church, from *Adam*, vntil the end of the world : and therfore compre-hends the *Law* of *Grace* alfo ; yea, all the Doctrine of God, contained in his Word. And this Law, is called the Law of the L O R D ; or if you will haue it, according to the Originalle :

Of יהוה, the Hebrew *Tetragramma-ton*, and the word *Iehovah.*

The *Law* of יְהֹוָה ; or , I H V H (if we may expreffe the Hebrew *Te-tragrammaton* in our letters.)

And thefe Characters, fome late
Inter-

Interpreters read *Iehouah*; ſuppoſing
the forme of that word , to imply
as much as ; *He that is, that was, and
that is to come.* For, ſay they ; *Ie,* *Reu.* 11. 17.
is a ſigne of the time to come. *Ieueth*;
Hee will bee, *Ho*, of the time pre-
ſent. *Hoveth*, hee that is. *Vah*, of
the time paſt. *Havah* , hee was.
Which wee will not denie to bee a
probable , and ingenious conceite :
but indeede, the word *Ichouah* , it
ſelfe; is not confeſſed to be ſo much
as heard of, to be an Hebrew word,
among the *Iewes* : neither doth it ſi-
gnifie any thing in that tongue. Nor
can we haue one Teſtimony, that
the Hebrew *Tetragrammaton* ; was
euer anciently ſo pronounced. And
therefore, vnleſſe we had better au-
thority, then probabilities , and vn-
certaine coniectures , of new Gra-
marians : I ſee no reaſon, why we
ſhould venter, to put this vnknowne
name vpon God. Which if it be the
right :

right : yet, not fo fufficiently warran-
ted, to be truely reuealed vnto vs ;
that we may vfe it, with the fame
confidence, wherewith we pro-
nounce the other names of God. As
you may fee more at large , in the
thirteenth Chapter , and third Se-
&tion of my *preparation to the Pfal-
ter.*

But, to teach vs then, that this *law*;
in which it is here faid, the bleffed
man delighteth ; is not the *law* of
man, but of God ; know that the vn-
pronounceable Hebrew word here
vfed (and infteede of which, the
Iewes fpoke *Adona*j, or *Elohim* ; the
Septuagint, and Apoftles, Κύριος : the
Ancient latine expofitors, *Dominus* ;
and the authorized englifh Tranfla-
tions, for the moft, LORD) is an effen-
tiall and vncommunicable name, of
our great, eternall, and euerliuing
God ; who is moft truely called, *Hee
that is, that was, and that is to come* :
and

and therefore, wherefoeuer you find this *Tetragrammaton*, יהוה. You may be aſſured, that there is to bee vnderſtood, eyther one, or all the Perſons of the ſacred Trinity. For, whereas the word, *Adonai*, and *Elohim*, are ſometime communicated to others; that is neuer ſo. And therfore, becauſe the word L O R D, by which wee (according to the Apoſtles) haue expreſt it; may be communicable to men: You ſhall vnderſtand; that, wherefoeuer in the laſt Engliſh tranſlation, you finde L O R D, thus in Capitall letters; there, is that glorious, and moſt eſſentiall name of God, to be vnderſtood; which neuer ought to be applied vnto any other.

But (which I had almoſt outſlipt) you muſt note that the holy-Ghoſt, vſeth here the word *Delight*; to ſhew vs further: that the deuotions of a bleſſed man; are not conſtrained, or ſeruile:

The meaning of the word *Delight.*

feruile : but rather, proceeding from a true and affectionate pleafure, in the worfhip of God, with the ftudie of his word. It muft be unto him, as it was to *Dauid : More to be defired then fine Gold ; and fweeter then honie, or the honie-combe.* Yea, the excellence of his affection ; is further, and another way manifefted ; in that hee is faid to meditate thereon , *Day* and *Night :* For, the *Day* and *Night,* in holy Scripture, hath a three-fold vnderftanding : *Temporall* ; *Morall* ; and *Allegoricall.* *Temporall,* is the day which wee enioy by the prefence of the Sunne : the night thereof, is that which is made by the abfence of the fame. *Morally,* it is taken for life and death ; Profperitie and aduerfity, or fuch like : and this is alfo *Metaphoricall. Allegorically,* the old *Law,* is called the Night ; and the *Gofpell,* tearmed the Day : and therefore *Zacharie* in his fong ; wherein he fpake of

Pfal. 19. 10.

Day & Night, what it fignifieth.

Gen. 1. 16.

of Chrift, and the light reuealed vn- *Luke* 1. 78. 79.
to Mankinde in the new Teftament,
faith ; that *The day-fpring from on high
hath vifited vs ; to giue light to them
that fit in darkneffe.* But Saint *Paul,*
writing vnto the *Romanes*, concer-
ning the faith of Chrift Jefus ; faith
in playner tearmes : *That the Night* *Rom.* 13. 12.
was paft, and the Day was at hand. E-
uen thus many waies, are the *Day*
and *Night* to be vnderftood, in the
booke of God. But in this place ;
they are to be confidered, according
to all and euery of thefe. The blef-
fed man ; meditateth on the Law of
the L O R D, *day* and *night* ; that is :
He pondereth all the mifteries of
Iefus Chrift ; as they were promifed,
figured, and prophecied of, in the
old *Teftament*, (which, as the *Night*,
fhadowed them ouer) and then be-
leeueth and confeffeth them, as they
were fulfilled in the new *Teftament* ;
which was the *Day* that made them
ap-

apparant to the whole world : Yea,
he is continually enclined vnto the
ftudy of *Piety*, without intermiffion ;
Morning and Euening, at Noone-
day and at Mid-night ; both in Pro-
fperity and Aduerfity ; Openly and
Secretly. For , many can bee
content, perhaps, to fpare fome lit-
tle time in the Day, for the meditati-
on of Gods word : but there are ve-
ry few, that will breake a fleepe ; and
arife at night, with *Dauid*, to praife
God : many can be content, whileft
they gayne any outward benefit, or
preferrement by their profeffion ; to
be hot and earneft in the ftudy there-
of : but few dare abide, the blacke
and terrible night of perfecution.
Nay, a little aduerfity, or worldly in-
conuenience, cooles all their zeale.
Hypocrites by *Day*, that is ; openly
in the eyes of the world ; will be ve-
ry forward, and feeme to be ftout
profeffors : but, in the *Night*, that is,
fecretly ,

ſecretly, and by themſelues; where none but God is witneſſe: they can laugh at their owne diſſembling; and with thoſe people, of whom God ſpeakes by the Prophet *Malachi*, they ſay thus: *It is in vaine to ſerue God; and what Profite is it that wee keepe his Commandements?* Againe, there be others, that by *Night*, with *Nicodemus*, dare, peraduenture, come to God; yet by *Day*, are affraid (or aſhamed) to be ſeene in a Religious mans company. But neyther of theſe, haue well vnderſtood what is ment by *Meditating* Gods word *Day* and *Night*: nor are they yet in the way of *Bleſſedneſſe.*

Out of this verſe; I doe obſerue theſe things. Firſt, that there is no true happineſſe, without the knowledge of God; and the continuall meditation of his word. And that thoſe, who are ſincerely adicted to his ſeruice, and the loue of his *Truth*, are

Mat. 3. 14.
Ob. 1.

are in the right way to *Bleſſedneſſe* ; howſoeuer Atheiſts, and worldly men, thinke them ſimple fooles ; and their ſtudy loſt labour.

2.

Secondly, I here note ; that he cannot promiſe to himſelfe, the reward of *Bleſſedneſſe* ; that frames a Religion, or way to ſerue God, out of his owne braine ; though neuer ſo ſtrict, or ſeeming holy : For, it muſt not be the Lawes, or traditions of men ; that, he muſt meditate, but the Law of the LORD.

3.

Laſtly, I doe here learne this Method, for the right ſtudy of *Diuinity* ; and practiſe of Chriſtianity. Firſt, that there muſt he a loue vnto the heauenly word : Secondly, a progreſſe, or going forward ; in the meditation thereof : and laſtly, ſuch a conſtant perſeuerance therein, from time to time, and at all times without limitation ; in ſo much, that there muſt bee ſome part of euery day and

and night, ſeparated for the ſeruice
of God ; that we may ſay with *Da-*
uid : *Euening, Morning, by Day, and at* Pſal. 55. 17.
Midnight, will I pray vnto thee.

 And, he ſhall be like a Tree planted, Verſe 3.
&c: Hauing deliuered in the two
former verſes, who is a Iuſt and bleſ-
ſed man, both by the *Negatiue*, and
Affirmatiue : he now confirmes his
former *propoſition* : Firſt, by a ſimi-
litude, taken from a fruitefull Tree,
euerlaſtingly greene : Secondly, by
the end, and proſperous ſucceſſe, of
all he takes in hand. By which illu-
ſtration, we may not imagine, that
they are compared with any intent
to be made equall (For, the bleſſed
eſtate of a good man, is farre beyond
all earthly compariſons) But by ſuch
knowne things, the holy-Ghoſt ap-
plies his demonſtrations to meane
capacities. And this kinde of tea-
ching, was vſuall with our *Sauiour* ;
as appeares by his illuſtration of
    F   *Faith* ;

Faith, and the *kingdome of Heauen,*
in likning it vnto a graine of *Muſtard-*
ſeede; or comparing Doﬄrine to
Leauen, and ſuch like. Nor hath it
beene negleﬄed among prophane
writers *:* For, a liuely Simily, is e-
ſteemed among all *Poets* (as well
ancient as moderne) to be one of the
principall ornaments of their *Poeſie.*
The Elegancy of whoſe *Poems,* ſome
haue not beene aſhamed to preferre,

Vide Epiſt.
Henr. Steph.
before *Mar-*
lorets com-
mentary vpon
the Pſalmes.

before theſe vnimitable *Odes :*
whereas, were they as learned in
theſe; as they would ſeeme to be in
the other (at leſt, if they could read
them with the ſame deſire and af-
feﬄion) they ſhould here finde; e-
uen, in the literall excellency; as
many rare, and admirable expreſſi-
ons. Obſerue well this firſt illuſtra-
tion; and ſee in what Author you can
better it.

For, although men may, for many
reſpeﬄs, be reſembled vnto Trees;
by

by reaſon of ſome ſimilitude in their
condition (as thus : Euery Tree is
eyther for building, or fire wood ;
and ſo, all men are eyther prepared
to build up the new *Ieruſalem* with-
all ; or, appointed fewell for hell
fire) yet ; there are certaine choyſe
Trees, which doe more properly
ſerue to figure out the eſtate of the
Bleſſed : as here in this Pſalme, and
by this compariſon ; you ſhall vnder-
ſtande.   For ; hereby, fiue things are
made remarkeable in the vpright
mans *happineſſe*.   Firſt, he is reſem-
bled vnto a Tree that is *planted*.   By
which, the ſtability, and certainty of
his eſtate is ſignified : For, as ſuch a
Tree ; is, where, by the carefulneſſe
and diligence of ſome gardener, or
husbandman ; he may be manured,
and preſerued from the choaking of
Thornes, and violence of beaſts ;
whilſt the wilde Trees of the For-
reſt, are euer in danger, of ſome ru-
ine :

F 2

Fiue things
obſeruable in
this illuſtrati-
on of a godly
mans happi-
neſſe.

He is Planted.

Pfal. 92.

ine : So, the iuft man, who in the Scripture is refembled vnto a *Palme* tree ; hath this fure and bleffed hope for his comfort : That God, who firft *planted* him ; will alfo protect him from being fpoyled of his leaues by the ftormes of aduerfitie ; or o-uerturned by the malice of the ad-uerfarie. When it fhall come to paffe, that (as Chrift faid) *Thofe plants*

Math. 15. 13.   *which his heauenly Father hath not planted, fhould be rooted vp.*

Moreouer, a Tree *planted* ; in-fteede of that wilde nature which formerly it retayned ; is bettered, and made more fruitefull by a new plantation : and in like manner ; that man, who had elfe beene naturally apt to bring forth nothing, but the fowre fruits of the flefh ; being plan-ted in the vine-yeard of Gods Church, by the hand of Grace : re-generates, and yeelds forth plenti-fully, the fweete fruits of the fpirit.

Second-

Secondly, it is planted by the *Springs, or Riuers of water*; by which, the bleſſedneſſe of the Iuſt man, is further illuſtrated : For, as that tree, can neither be barren thorough the ſterrile drought of the ſoyle ; nor endangered by the ſcorching heate of Sommer: whoſe roote is euer moiſtened, with the nouriſhing waters of a pleaſant ſtreame ; So, the regenerate man, hauing his roote in Chriſt *(* where the euer ſpringing fountaines of his Grace ; with ſweete dewes of mercy, continually cheriſh it) euen he, ſhall alway flouriſh. For, neither can he be conſumed as the wicked are, by the burning fire of Gods indignation ; nor made vnprofitable for want of nouriſhment. To the ſame effect ſpeakes the Prophet *Ieremy*, in his illuſtration of ſuch a mans happineſſe ; by a ſimilitude taken from the like Tree. *He ſhall bee* (ſaith he) *as a Tree that is planted by*

Secondly, he is placed by the Riuers of water.

Ierem. 17. 18.

F 3   *the*

*the waters ; and that spreadeth forth
her rootes by the Riuer, and shall not see
when heate commeth : but her leafe
shall be greene, and shall not be carefull
in the yeere of drouth, neither shall ceafe
from yeelding fruite.* By the *Riuers*

The Riuers of waters, what they meane.

of water, in this *Pfalme,* is Allegorically meant ; the word of God, and his Sacraments : which, are the means whereby he infufeth into vs, the graces of his Spirit ; keepes vs growing in Faith ; and nourisheth fruits, to eternall life.

Thirdly, it *giueth fruite in due fea-*

Thirdly, he is fruitfull, and that in feafon.

fon : Whereby is manifested another propertie of the bleffed Iuftman : *By the fruite* (faith our Saui-our) *the Tree is knowne :* and fo is the iuft man by his workes : Who, in bringing forth his fpirituall fruits, may (not vnfitly) be refembled to a Tree. For, as the Tree brings forth fruits for others, rather then for it felfe : So, the vpright man fructi-fies fics, and ſends forth good workes, and deedes of Charitie; not, thereby to merit ought for himſelfe; but to glorifie God, and to benefit others. Which is a noble *Bleſſedneſſe.* For, as the Apoſtle ſaith; *it is a more bleſ-ſed thing to giue, then to receiue.* Further; we haue the Pronoune *His:* to ſhew vs, that as the Tree giueth forth no fruite but his owne, and according to his kinde; So, the *righteous,* doth the workes proper to a regenerate man; all the good deedes which he performeth, are done with that which is his owne: and ſo cherefully; that they may be called *His.* Yea, he yeeldeth forth good fruits, according to the meaſure, and qualitie of thoſe gifts which he hath receiued. Laſtly, the Tree giueth forth her fruite *in ſeaſon,* or in time: that is; in her time of fruitfulneſſe; and ſo; the vpright man, doth good in due time; euen vpon the

F 4   firſt

Acts. 20.

The pronoun *His.*

When, fruit is giuen in ſeaſon, or in time

Exercises vpon

firſt occaſion offered. He is neuer bar-
ren, when neceſſity requires fruit. If
in one day, a thouſand men neede
his comforting hand ; he is euer wil-
ling, according to his ability, to giue
redreſſe vnto them all. Neyther too
ſoone, nor too late comes his chari-
ty : but, like ſweete and well ripened
fruite, is euer, then ready to be recei-
ued ; when it may be moſt accepta-
ble to God, timely, in reſpect of him-
ſelfe ; and very profitable to others.

Fruit, what it
ſignifieth.

But indeede, by the *fruit* here is prin-
cipally meant Faith, and the confeſ-
ſion of ſaluation by Chriſt : which can
neuer be, without workes. And that
is it, which our *Saviour meant*, when

Ioh. 15. 8.

hee ſaid : *Herein is my Father glorified,
that you beare much fruit.*

Fourthly He is
euer flouriſh-
ing.

Fourthly, *His leafe ſhall not fade :*
Yet ; the ſimilitude holds very pro-
perly, in that the *bleſſed* man is re-
ſembled vnto a tree, not onely fruit-
full, but flouriſhing alſo ; and euer a-
dorned

dorned with the comely ornament of greene leaues. For, as the *Palme-tree*, whereto the Iuſt man is likened, in the 92 *Pſalme* (and from which tree, it is very likely, this ſimilitude was taken) is neuer, as *Pliny* ſaith, without fruit ; and therefore muſt, conſequently, bee alwayes greene : ſo, the Iuſt man is continually beau-tified, with all the accompliſhments of a Chriſtian ; full of holy thoughts, plentifull in profitable words, and ſeriouſly exerciſed in good actions, without wearineſſe in well-doing : and to accompany that fruitfulneſſe, enioyeth ſuch a perpetuall happines, as growes at no time ſubiect to any momentary change. What ſtorm ſo-euer happens, hee is ſtill in a flouri-ſhing and proſperous eſtate : yea, when the vngodly (like thoſe trees which are altered, according to the diſpoſition of euery ſeaſon) muſt loſe, in the winter of their triall, all that

Plin. lib. 16. *cap.* 20.

that vncertaine glory, gotten in the ſpring-time of their proſperity : euen then ; the happineſſe of the righteous is ſo permanent, as the coldeſt froſt of aduerſity, can neuer ſtrip him of his faire leaues : that is : no perſecuti-on ſhall bee able to take from him, the faire liuery of his profeſſion, nor put him, beſide the Crowne of an immortall glory.

5. What euer hee doth, proſpers.

Fiftly, *whatſoeuer he doth, ſhall pro-ſper* : In theſe words, hee doth (as it were) ſumme vp, and make perfect his expreſſion of *happineſſe.* And the *Prophet* doth it without the *Meta-phor* ; for, I haue obſerued, that to expreſſe one and the ſame ſentence ; partly by the figure, and partly with-out : is ordinary in the *Pſalmes.* Yet, the great Scholler, and Cardinall, *Bellarmine*; in his Comment vpon this *Pſalme,* would haue theſe words (*whatſoeuer hee doth ſhall proſper*) to be referred vnto the *Tree.* Then, ha-uing

uing interpreted the Hebrew Verbe,
Iaſtiach ; *proſperare faciet*, will make
to proſper : he gathers from thence,
an active vertue to bee in the tree ;
helping on the ripening of his owne
fruits. And, by the application of the
ſimilitude, would alſo note vnto vs ;
that, there were an active vertue of
free will in man, concurring with the
Diuine grace, to meritorious works.
But, by his leaue, it ſeemes to mee,
not ſo to bee vnderſtood ; for, that
interpretation, is both harſh in the
ſence, and contradictory to the opi-
nion of moſt Expoſitors. Yea, one
of his owne faction, *Lorinus*, a lear-
ned *Ieſuite*, writing on this *Pſalme*,
ſayth ; that it ought rather to be vn-
derſtood of the *Iuſt man*, then of the
Tree. *Lyra*, a very ancient Expoſi-
tor, hath ſo taken it alſo : and ſo haue
the greateſt number of moſt authen-
ticall Writers. For which cauſe ; I ra-
ther allow it : but eſpecially, by rea-
ſon

ſon I beleeue it, to be indeed the beſt, and natural ſence of this Text ; agreeable to the happy eſtate of a good man ; and the ſame bleſſing, which the *Scriptures* teſtifie, to haue bcene vouchſafed to ſuch as feare God.

Geneſ. 39.

For, it is ſayd of *Ioſeph* : *The* L O R D *made all that he did, to proſper in his hands.*

A Caueat.

But from hence, wee muſt neither gather, that all thoſe are good men, who proſper, and thriue, in the things of this life ; neither imagine, it is hcere promiſed, that the Righteous ſhall bee without troubles, or hinderances, in their temporall affaires. The meaning rather is : that al things, (euen thoſe) wherein they ſeeme to the world moſt miſerable, ſhould redound to their comfort; and proſper them in the way to eternall life.

Rom. 8. 28.

According to the ſaying of S. *Paul* ; *All things worke together for good, to them that loue God.* *Dauid* alſo confirmeth

firmeth the fame, out of his owne
experience : for, faith he ; *It was good
for mee, that I was in trouble.* And in-
deede, it is the end which crownes
all, and that which makes the vnder-
taking profperous, or vnfortunate :
not the occurrences, that happen
well, or ill, in the proceeding. For,
though a *Commander* in the warres
finde, that all his determinations pro-
ceeded ill, in the ordering of his Bat-
tles ; and that all his *Stratagems*, tur-
ned a while, to his hinderance : yea,
though with the loffe, of many thou-
fands of his men, and the effufion of
much of his owne bloud, he hath en-
dured a terrible, and fharp encoun-
ter. Yet, if at laft, the victory bee on
his fide, he hath his aime ; and thinks,
that his vndertaking profpered in his
hands. So, though a Chriftian man
hath, in this life, fuffered innumera-
ble miferies ; though matters haue
fucceeded fo ill with him, that for-
row

row vpon forrow, and mifcheefe vp-
on mifcheefe, ouerwhelmed him, and
euery thing that he endeauoured, fell
out contrary to his expectation ; yet,
if at laft (as queftionleffe he fhall) he
reape the Crowne of immortall glo-
ry : we may very well fay, that *what-
foeuer he did, hath profpered.* Yea, his
miferies and infirmities, were for his
good, fuffered to come vpon him ;
euen they alfo, profpred in his hands ;
and were the meanes to make him,
a right bleffed man.

Bleffedneffe, two-fold.
Luke 14. 15.

For, you muft vnderftand, that
there is a two-fold *Bleffedneffe* ; *Bea-
titudo in via, & in Regno* ; A bleffed-
neffe in the *way*, and in the *Kingdom*.
That in the *way*, is alfo two-fold ;
one, on the right hand ; and the o-
ther, on the left : The *left-hand* hap-
pineffe ; is the abundance of tempo-
rall profperities. For, the *Pfalmift*
hauing reckoned vp many temporall
benefits ; concludeth with thefe
words.

words. *Bleſſed are the people, that bee* *Pſal.* 144. 15.
ſo. Happineſſe on the *right hand,* is
the gift of ſpirituall graces, beſtowed
in this life. For, ſaith our Sauiour, *Matth.* 5.
*Bleſſed are the poore in ſpirit, the hum-
ble ; thoſe that hunger and thirſt after
rightcouſneſſe,* &c. But the laſt of
theſe *bleſſings* ; appertaines onely to
the children of God : the other, are
indifferently beſtowed, both on
good and bad.

   The *Bleſſedneſſe* in the *Kingdome* ;
is that, which is principally meant
in this *Pſalme* : and indeede, the
moſt perfect compleat happineſſe.
The poſſeſſion of that, wee haue
now in hope onely. None, but the
ſonnes of God, can enioy it, in the
other world (as is aforeſayd) nor,
can any man, but thoſe that haue
their hearts enlarged, by the Holy
Ghoſt ; enter into a worthy thought
thereof, here. For, as S. *Paul* ſaith ; *It* 1 *Cor.* 2. 9.
is that, which eye hath not ſeene, nor
                  eare

eare heard, neither comes it into the heart of man, to conceiue what God hath prepared for them, that love him. It is fo many degrees, beyond the felicity of this life, that the moft bleffed man is miferable here, in comparifon of the happineffe, which hee fhall bee crowned with all, after his death. And therfore, if you haue refpeét to that, which may moft properly bee called *Bleffedneffe*, it muft bee loked for in another world ; for, as the *Poet* faith :

———— *Diciq. beatus Ante obitum nemo, fupremaq. funera debet.*

We none may bleffed call, Before their funerall.

What makes perfeét Bleffedneffe.

But, becaufe carnall men, are too too much perfwaded, that true felicity may bee enioyed in this life ; I would

would haue them learne, what is re-
quired, to the making vp of a perfect
Bleſſedneſſe. For, they muſt know,
there are three things, which are of
the eſſence of true felicity. The firſt
is, the knowledge of the *Cheefe Good*; *Ioh.* 17. 13.
this is eternal life, to know the only true
God, and him whom thou haſt ſent, Ie-
ſus Chriſt, faith S. *Iohn.* Secondly,
there muſt be a fruition, and full en-
ioying of that *Cheefe Good,* being ſo
knowne. And laſtly, a perfect de-
light, and contentation in that which
is enioyed. Without euery of which
circumſtances, there is no perfect
happineſſe. For, hee that enioyes,
and is contented; without the full
knowledge, of the certainty, and
worth of that, which he enioyes : hath
but a dull vncertaine contentation ;
and is depriued of a great part of his
felicity.

In like manner, hee that knowes
what it is to bee happy, and hath it

G   not

not in poſſeſſion, is ſo farre from happineſſe; that he is the more miſerable, by the apprehenſion which he hath, of the great good hee wanteth. But if hee did know, and enioy to; yet, if hee had not the bleſſing of a contented minde, it were as much, as if he enioyed nothing.

S. *Auguſtine* hath a ſpeech, much to this purpoſe, in his firſt Booke, *De-Moribus Eccleſiæ Catholicæ*: For, ſaith he, *Beatus neque ille (quantum exiſtimo) dici poteſt, qui non habet quod amat qualecunq̃. ſit*; *neq̃. qui habet quod amat, ſi noxium ſit*; *neq. qui non amat quod habet, etiamſi optimum ſit.* That is: *Neither, as I thinke, can hee bee ſayd, to be bleſſed, who enioyeth not what hee loueth, whatſoeuer it be*; *nor hee, that attaineth to what hee affecteth, if it bee hurtfull*; *nor hee, that is not pleaſed with that, which he poſſeſſeth, although it bee the beſt thing.* And hee giueth this reaſon: *Nam, & qui appetit quod adipiſci*

adipiſci non poteſt cruciatur ; & qui ad-
eptus eſt, quod appetendum non eſt, fal-
litur ; & qui non appetit quod adipiſcen-
dum eſſet ; ægrotat. Id eſt : *For hee*
which deſireth what cannot be attained,
is vexed ; hee that hath attained vnto
that, which proues not worthy deſiring,
is deceiued ; and hee which affecteth
not, what is indeede worthy the enioy-
ing, is ſicke ; or faulty in himſelf. And
ſo, not one of theſe, can bee bleſſed :
becauſe, neither of their ſoules is
without vexation and miſery.   For,
if it might bee ſo ; theſe two contra-
ries, *Bleſſedneſſe,* and *Vnhappineſſe* ;
ſhould dwell together at the ſame
time, in one man : which were im-
poſſible.

This *Bleſſedneſſe,* cannot then, con-
ſiſt in temporall & tranſitory things.
For, though we may haue the know-
ledge of their vtmoſt good, & get alſo
the poſſeſſion of them ; yet, it is im-
poſſible, they ſhould giue vs a con-

True bleſſed-
neſſe conſi-
ſteth not in
temporall
things.

G 2   tent,

tent, beyond which, nothing is to be defired. For, the foule of man, is of a fpirituall nature; and of fo large an apprehenfion, that the whole world is not able to fill it. Though you fhould feede the boundleffe defire of man, with Kingdome vpon Kingdome; hee would neuer finde end of defiring, vntill hee had the poffeffion of the whole world, with all the creatures therein: and though he could compaffe that: yet, becaufe the mortalitie of his body, would euer put him in feare, to be depriued therof; he would neuertheleffe be full of difquiet. Nay, were it poffible, that feare, might be taken away alfo: it would then difcontent him, that there were not more worlds, & new things, to couet and poffeffe. And fo, he would bee vnhappy, in the middeft of all that happineffe.

Ecclef. I. 17.   This, made *Soloman* fay (when he had fearched into the nature of all creatures,

creatures, and ſought to pleaſe his ſoule, in whatſoeuer it longed for) that all things vnder the Sunne (euen knowledge, and thoſe which are ac-counted the beſt) were vanity, and vexation of ſpirit. And this, if world-ly men did better conſider, doubt-leſſe, they would not ſo much adict themſelues to the things of this life : but ſeeke to haue their ſoules, rather filled with the knowledge of God ; who is only able to ſatisfie them, & without whom, they are euer empty, and ſeeking vp and downe for that, which ſhould fill them. For, the end to which God created the ſoule of man, was (as *S. Auguſtine* ſaith) That ſhe might know him ; in know-ing, loue him ; and in louing, enioy him : wherein conſiſteth perfect *bleſ-ſedneſſe*, neuer to be loſt againe ; and that, which is principally meant in this *Pſalme.*

The *Doctrines*, that we may gather

from this third verfe, are thefe.

Doct. 1.   Firft, that if the *Bleſſed* are plan-
ted, & not as naturally growing trees :
then, the efficient caufe of our falua-
tion, is God. For, it is of his graci-
ous fauour, that we are planted in the
Vineyard of his Church ; otherwife,
wee had beene, as wilde Oliue-
trees, growing on the barren moun-
taines.

Doct. 2.   Secondly, in that it is fayd. The
Bleffed is as the Tree, planted *by the
riuers of waters :* Wee are taught,
what the inftrumentall caufes of our
faluatiō are ; euen the Word of God
& his bleffed Sacraments. For, by the

What the Ri-
uers of wa-
ters fignifie.
Springs, or *Riuers of waters*, are thofe
allegorically vnderftood (as I fayd
before) & in that, they are fayd to be
planted ; thereby, wee alfo gather
further, that fuch as are out of the
Church, till they bee there feated, by
the fountaines of (life and inocula-
ted into the myfticall body of *Chriſt*)
                       are

are not yet in the ſtate of *Bleſſed-neſſe.*

Doct. 3.

Thirdly, wee may hereby know, whether wee belong to God, or no. For, if wee bee trees of his Vineyard, wee cannot but bee ſenſible, of the ſweet graces and operations of his Spirit : and ſhall not be found barren, of thoſe ſpirituall fruits, which God wil looke for, in their due time. And be aſſured, that if wee bee vnprofita-ble ; though wee carry neuer ſo many faire leaues of hypocriſie, to couer our ſterility : we ſhal one day bee ſtript of them, and caſt into the fire.

Doct. 4.

Fourthly and laſtly, wee are here taught, not to iudge of men, by their proſperity, or aduerſity ; but, how-ſoeuer their outward affaires ſuc-ceede, to eſteeme them bleſſed, and happy men, that loue and honour God. And ſo, I conclude this firſt part of the *Pſalme,* which doth in breefe deliuer thus much : *That hee,*

G 4 *which*

which would be a bleſſed man, ought to
auoyd all manner of ſinne, loue Gods
Word: meditate it, practiſe it, goe for-
ward in that practiſe, bring forth
fruits of rightcouſneſſe ; and
continue vnto the end
of his life, in that
courſe.

The

The ſecond part of the
P S A L M E.

4. **T**He *vngodly are not
ſo : but are like the
Chaffe ,   which   the
winde driueth away.*

5. *Therefore the vngodly ſhall
not ſtand in the iudgement, nor ſin-
ners in the Congregation of the righ-
teous.*

6. *For,   the* L O R D *know-
eth the way of the righteous : but
the way of the vngodly ſhall pe-
riſh.*

The

Ver. 4.

THe Prophet ; or, rather the Holy-Ghoſt, by the mouth of the Prophet, hauing in the former part of this Pſalme ; in an excellent manner, ſet downe vnto vs the bleſſed eſtate of a good Chriſtian ; and in diuers particulars diſcouered, and illuſtrated his matchleſſe *Bleſſedneſſe* ; that we might be thereby drawne to loue and ſeeke it. Doth now, in this other part, briefly (yet as fully) acquaint vs with the miſerable condition of the vnbeleeuing ſinner. euen in theſe few words : *The vngodly are not ſo.* For, they carrie in them a direct *Antitheſis* vnto the whole firſt part of the *Pſalme*; and imply euery whit aſmuch, as if the Prophet had ſaid : *The wicked are ſuch*; as neyther diſcontinue their *walke*, in the *Counſels* of the *vngodly* : nor ſhunne the *way* of *euill doers* ; nor auoide the *ſeate* of the *ſcornefull.* And therefore, are in no poſſibility, to be
ſo

ſo happy as are the righteous. And
this the *Septuagint*, very powerfully
expreſſeth, by doubling the Nega-
tiue, οὐκ οὕτως οἱ ἀσεβεῖς, οὐκ οὕτως, *the wic-
ked are nor ſo, nor ſo.* To wit: nor ſo
holy in their life; nor ſo bleſſed in
their end. They are not ſo ſtudious
of Gods word, as the righteous; and
therefore he taketh no ſuch know-
ledge of their waies: they doe not ſo
affect the *way* of his feruice; & there-
fore he ſuffers their *way* to periſh: they
are not ſo *planted*; and therefore not
ſo ſafe, but in danger to be rooted
vp, by the iudgements of God: they
are not ſo ſituated, where they may
be nouriſhed, by the moyſture of the
Riuers of Gods grace, conueyed by
his word and Sacraments, into their
hearts; and therefore, not ſo flouri-
ſhing; but in danger to be withered
by the burning heate of his Indigna-
tion: they are not ſo fruitfull; and
therefore, likely to vndergoe a curſe,
with

The diſſimili-
tude that is
betweene the
wicked, and
the righteous.

with the barren fig-Tree. They are in nothing anfwerable to the condition of the well planted Tree, here fpoken of: but vngodly men, and Hypocrites, for the moft part, yeeld no fruit at all. If they bring forth any; it is not good. And then it is no better then if they were vnfruitfull : *Math. 3. 10. For euery Tree that bringeth not forth good fruite, fhall be hewen downe, and caft into the fire.* Or though it might, perhaps, for fome refpects, be called good fruite, which they giue; then it is none of their owne : For, they doe, like moft of the great rich men in thefe dayes ; who, other while indeede, relieue a few poore foules. But it is with the fruit of other mens labours. Yea, they leaue many goodly fhewes of Charity behinde them ; with that which had beene, with extreme couetoufneffe and oppreffion, torne, as it were, out of the throates of their poore Neighbours.

bours. Or if we ſhould grant that it was their owne fruite they gaue ; yet, it would be found to come out of ſeaſon, and when there is no great neede of it : whereas a cup of cold water ; giuen unto a poore man in extremity : comes in better ſeaſon, then a great deale of vaine liberality at other times. But, if wee ſhould yeeld them this ; that their fruite came in *ſeaſon* ; it is in their owne *ſeaſon* then : And when is that ? Forſooth, now and then ; perhaps at ſuch times, when as the cuſtomes of their Countrie require publike hoſpitality. And then ; it is but forc't, ſowre, and unſauorie fruite. For, moſt commonly, for one honeſt man that ſhall ſatisfie his neceſſity among them ; two Ruffians ſhall be made drunke. Or elſe their *ſeaſon* is, when they may take occaſion to make moſt ſhew to the world, of the ſeeming good they doe : like the *Phari-ſies,*

The World-lings ſeaſon in which hee brings fruite.

Math. 6. 2.

fies, that blew Trumpets, when they gaue almes. But indeede, the principall time and feafon of their vintage is; when the Axe is fet vnto the roote of the Tree. Then; when the leaues of their youth, and profperity are fallen off; the branches quite withered; the bodie rotten, ready to ftinke with putrifaction; and they in cafe no more to hoard vp, or keepe it vnto themfelues; then (if the *Diuell* doe not come before they be aware, and carry them away by the Rootes; as fometime he fcrueth old Trees in the Forreft) it may fo fall out, that they leaue a few vnfeafonable fruits behind them : which often, in fine painted Almefhoufes; make fhew of more reliefe, then is halfe performed.

Nor are the vngodly, in refpect of their vnfruitfulneffe, or vntimelineffe in bearing fruite (onely) fo contrary to the righteous : but euen their

leaues,

leaues, thoſe their faire leaues ; that
make them ſeeme ſo flouriſhing, are
but the Sommer ornaments of pro-
ſperity ; and muſt wither and fall off,
in the winter of their triall. Yea,
nothing they take in hand ſhall proſ-
per them in the way to true happi-
neſſe ; therefore all their vnderta-
kings are in vaine. And as the holy-
Ghoſt here ſaith : *It is nothing ſo with
them*, as with the Godly.

Thus ; exceeding elegantly, hath
the Prophet deſcribed the miſery of
the wicked, by oppoſing it vnto the
felicitie of the Iuſt. Which he yet
maketh more apparant : and, how-
ſoeuer the world eſteemes her owne
as fortunate men ; he ſhewes the
contrary. Seeming alſo, not conten-
ted to ſet it forth by a ſimilitude, di-
rectly contrarie to the former ; he
leaueth the firſt Metaphor, and re
ſembles them, to the vileſt and ligh-
teſt *Chaffe* : as if elſe, he ſhould not
haue

haue made them contemptible e-
nough, in his expreffion.

    And here I could fhew, how pro-
perly the wicked may, for diuerfe
reafons, be likened unto *Chaffe*. As
in regard of that lightneffe, which
makes them inconftantly carried a-
way, with euery vanity : or in re-
fpeft of their fterility, with fuch like.
Which (becaufe euery reafonable ca-
pacity can apprehend them) I will o-
mit : & only defire you to take from
hence this obferuation. To wit, that
the enemies, and oppreffors of Gods
Children ; with all other vngodly
men (though they be admired of the
world, and feeme mighty and vnmo-
uable in their owne haughty opini-
ons) are, (neuertheles indeed) poore
bafe things ; meere *Chaffe*. Nay,
the worft and lighteft of it : euen
that which is fcattered euery way
with the winde. Or worfe, if worfe
may be : For, they are not onely
vn-

**Why the wic-
ked are refem-
bled to *Chaffe*.**

vnſetled, and reſtleſly driuen too and
fro, in their owne vaine practiſes ; or
tumbled vp and downe by the diſ-
tempered furie of their miſerable af-
fections : but their riches, honours,
powers, and *their very place of being*
(as *Dauid* ſaith) *ſhall decay, and be no
more found.* For, the terrible winde
of Gods wrath, ſhall puffe all, in-
to euerlaſting perdition. Yea ,
Gods iudgement will ruſh vpon
them on a ſuddaine, and inuiſibly,
as a wind : which ſhall come they
know not from whence ; and carrie
them they know not whether. Nor
ſhall their ſtrength, eminence, or
greatneſſe, defend them. But, as the
winde makes moſt hauock among
tall Cedars, on high Mountaines :
So, ſhall their pride and loftineſſe,
make them more ſubiect to the tem-
peſt of Gods indignation. As appea-
red in *Pharaoh, Nebuchadonezor, He-
rod* ; and ſuch other. But ſome may

H   ſay

fay; many vngodly men liue free from all thofe miferies and croffes here fpoken off. Truely, it feemes fo for a time; but the greater will be their forrow at the laft. Nay, I am perfwaded, that euen in this life, and at the beft; they haue fo much bit-

The vnhappy-nes of world-ly men in this life.

terneffe, to make vnfauorie all their delights : as, if we could look into the hearts and confciences, of thofe that feeme happieft men to the world-ward. I beleeue we fhould difcouer fo much horror, and difquietneffe; as would make vs fet light by our difcontentments. For, many of them, amid their aboundance of wealth and honours ; are more dif-tempered with toyes ; then a conftant Chriftian is, with his greateft afflicti-ons. And if trifles will not moue them ; they haue matters of greater confequence to difturbe their reft. One grieues, to fee the familie, which he thought to make honourable, by his

his owne pollicy ; quite rooted out by the improuidence of his Children : Yea, the miſerable Catiue, liues to behold his ſonnes prodigalitie, conſume his vſury ; and yet hath not the power to afford himſelfe the benefit of his owne labours, neither to doe one good deede, that may purchaſe a prayer for him ; untill it is too late. Another, hath labour'd for the applauſe of the people ; and with vexation of ſpirit, comes to heare his name made the iuſt ſubiect of Libels ; and himſelfe reputed odious in the common-wealth. One, is ſicke, for ſome diſgrace receiued from his Prince. A ſecond, grieued with the vnkindenes of thoſe whom he thought his beſt friends. A third, mad at the pride of his equall. A fourth, ready to hang himſelfe for the inſolence of his inferiour. A fift, pines with enuying at his ſuperiour. A ſixt, ſleepes not for deſire of pre-

H 2　　　ferment.

ferment. A feauenth, trembles through feare of lofing his office. The eighth, hath a wife that is more fhame, and difcontent vnto him, then all thefe. And, which is worfe then that too; he knowes not what fhall become of him at laft. For, fometime he thinkes that men die like beafts, without hope of another life. And then, it grieues him, that he muft for euer, leaue the world, which he fo much loued. Another while, he remembers he hath heard of a *God*; and *a Day of Iudgement.* Which, putteth him into fuch a defperat feare; that he is neuer alone, but his heart quakes; and his guilty Confcience fo ftings & threatens him, with hell and damnation; that hee fometime wifheth hee were indeede, realy *duft,* or *Chaffe*; and that, the winde might fcatter him into nothing.

Oh God! that I were able fo to ferue
this

*this, into the hearts of worldlings; as to
make their muddy apprehenſions, more
ſenſible of their vnhappineſſe: and
allure them, to ſeeke for that true
and perfeЄt felicitie, which is here pro-
miſed. But alas! it is beyond my po-
wer. For the whole world (almoſt)
hath runne through all the degrees of
wickedneſſe; and the greateſt part, are
become* Benchers, *in that damnable
ſociety of* Scorners: *with whom, it is
impoſsible to preuaile. Nay, my God;
would thou mightſt bee pleaſed
(though it were but ſo farre, to ena-
ble mee with thy ſpirit) that the ap-
prehenſion of theſe things, might e-
uer continue in my ſelfe, ſo feruent,
as at ſometimes they be. For, by that
meanes, I ſhould not onely; neuer more
againe, be carried away by thoſe vanities
and infirmities, whereunto youth and
the frailty of my condition is prone;
but become alſo, ſo highly delighted
with the contemplation, and hope*

H 3   of

of that incomparable bleſſedneſſe which
is prepared for the louers of thy Law :
that the worlds minions ſhold ſee, I did
not meerely in word ; but truely in
deede ; negleɛt, and deſpiſe all thoſe
things, which they account either feli-
cities, or diſaſters in this life. Yea, they
ſhould perceiue me, ſo farre from thin-
king my ſelfe a miſerable man ; For
being in pouerty, ſlandered, negleɛted,
contemned, tortured with ſuch like : or,
from imagining my ſelfe a happy man,
in the fruition of that vaine fauour,
honour, wealth, caſe, fame, and reſpeɛt,
which they glorie in : as, they ſhould with
enuie be forced to confeſſe within them-
ſelues ; that, by a meanes which the
world knew not, I had ariued at ſuch
felicitie ; as in reſpeɛt thereof, their
happineſſe, was but as dirt, and dung
to Gold and Siluer. And perhaps alſo
when they were in their greateſt earth-
ly pompe : It ſhould more vexe them, to
behold me (whom they account miſera-
ble)

ble) difdayning thofe things as triuiall,
wherein they place their higheft blef-
fedneffe; then it can delight, or content
them, to poffeffe thofe pleafures or pre-
ferments which they enioy. This, oh Lord
were pofsible; if thou wouldft alwaies
prefcrue in thy feruant, the confiderati-
on, which at fometime thou vouchfafeft
to beftow vpon me. But I am the mea-
neft of thy children; and I confeffe that
thefe good affections, and apprehenfions,
which I fometime haue of the bleffed-
neffe here promifed: doe often; yea, too
often faile in me. And then, I doe not
onely fhrinke as much as any other, vn-
der the burthen of temporall afflictions:
but my heart is alfo intangled, with
thofe defires, and prepofterous con-
tentments, that vaineft world-lings
feeke after. Which weakeneffe; I both
heartily pray thee (Oh God) to heale in
me; and furely beleeue alfo, that thou
wilt doe it, when it fhall be moft for thy
glory, and my furtherance, in the way

H 4   of

of *trueſt* Bleſſedneſſe. *The thought whereof; hath now ſo highly tranſported me; that, I had almoſt forgotten what I had more to ſay, touching the infelicity of the wicked.* But now I deſcend againe, to ſpeake of them.

Verſe. 5.

Therefore the vngodly ſhall not ſtand in the Iudgement, &c. You haue formerly beene giuen to vnderſtand, of the great difference, that is betweene the *Righteous* and the *vngodly*; both in their condition, and their reward. Now, he ſhewes that a difference will be betwixt them ; not in this life only : but alſo in the laſt day. For, that is the principal *Iudgement* here ment : and ſpoken of, *per Antonomaſiam*, as the *Arabick* Interpreter, by theſe words, *in fine*, doth plainely denote.

To ſtand, what it ſignifies.

They ſhall not be able to ſtand in the iudgment, nor in the congregatian of the righteous.

That is ; they ſhall not be approued but haue iudgement pronounced againſt

againſt them, to their ouerthrow, at
the generall *Doome.* For, ſo are theſe
words, *ſhall not ſtand,* to bee vnder-
ſtood. And the phraſe is not onely
proper to the *Hebrewes*; but vſuall
among the *Latines,* and vs alſo.
Cicero hath, *Cauſa cadere*; which, is
after the ſame manner of ſpeaking:
And *Terence,* where hee ſaith, *Se, vix
ſtetiſſe*; meanes that ſome of his Fa-
bles were ſcarſe approued of, by the
common people. And when, with
vs, a man comes to his triall, before a
Iudge: we often ſay, *Hee cannot ſtand
out.* Or, that, *Hee will haue a fall*;
when we meane, his cauſe ſhall not
receiue approbation.

Now, the reaſon, why *the vn-
godly ſhall not ſtand in Iudgement,*
&c. is partly ſhewn in the for-
mer verſe. And that is, becauſe
they are but as the *Chaffe*; euen the
refuſe of man-kind, vaine, light, vnne-
ceſſary perſons, without fruit, whol-
ly

ly voyd of that worth and weight, which fhould make them of efteeme in the fight of God. Yea, fuch as cannot bee able to endure his iudgements ; becaufe, they will bee vnto them, *as the winde, fcattering Chaffe.* Alas! who would imagine this (feeing the brauery of this worlds Fauorites) but that the Spirit of God hath fayd it ? Now, they are fo mighty, that they thinke it impoffible, to bee mooued. They haue *Counfells*, in which the *Righteous* are not to *walke :* *Wayes* , wherein they muft not *ftand: Iudgements,* in which the innocent dare not appeare : And they haue Affemblies, and folemne meetings, from which they exclude all good men. But, when the Iudgement here fpoken of, comes (for there will come fuch a day) the poore difperfed, and defpifed members of *Chrift,* fhall bee gathered into one *Congregation,* whereinto no vncleane thing

thing ſhall enter. Nor, ſhall the vn-
godly mingle among them, in their
Aſſembly ; but bee ſeparated from
them, and thruſt vnto the left hand
of the Iudge. And although, here
they may appeare powerfull ; make
great boaſt of their authority; and,
perhaps, in our Courts of Iudge-
ment on earth, be able to ſtand out,
vntill they haue ruined the innocent
(for, in any cauſe, fauours are to bee
had, among the corrupted Iudges of
this world.) Yet, in the generall
Doome, when euery man ſhall ap-
peare naked, without bribes ; and
before a Iudge, that can neuer be cor-
rupted. Alas! what will thoſe things?
thoſe vain things, profit them, wherin
they now glory? Then, thoſe noble
Tyrants ſhall be glad, to ſneake into
corners, and cranies of the earth, to
hide themſelues from the preſence
of God. They ſhall not haue power,
to ſtand among thoſe poore men, o-
uer

uer whom they haue heretofore ty-
rannized ; nor bee able to abide the
leaft triall of Gods Iuftice : but, af-
frighted with the terrible afpe&t of
their angry Iudge, and tortured with
the horrours of an accufing confci-
ence ; fhall be vtterly amazed, deie-
&ted, confounded, and with a diftra-
&ted feare, be glad (& in vain be glad)
to intreat the hills, that they would
fall down, and couer them. That you
may be confident, of the terror of
this Iudgement ; & that, there will be
a feparation of the wicked, from the
Congregation of the righteous (as it
is here fayd) See, what our Sauiour
Matth. 25.   fpeaketh, in the 25 chapter of Saint
Matthewes Gofpell, to this purpofe.

What Iudge-
ment the Ho-
ly Ghoft mea-
neth in this
Pfalm.

But, this place may haue refpe&t to
other *Iudgements*. For, befide that
great and generall *Doome*; there
is a two-fold Iudgement, in this life :
wherein the *wicked fhall not bee able to
ftand*. One is, the *Iudgement* of them-
felues,

felues; when their owne confcience fhall accufe; and condemning them as guilty, caft them downe headlong into defpaire. The other is, when the plagues and iudgements of God are fuffered, to lay hold of them in this world, for the example of others. Now, in neither of thefe; fhall they be able to ftand out before God.

Note here, that thofe Hebrew words, which are interpreted in our Tranflation, *They fhall not ftand*, are in the *Septuagint*, and vulgar La-tine Taanflations, turned thus, οὐκ αὐαςήσοὐ, *Non refurgunt*, that is, *They rife not againe.* And thence, fome haue weakly and ignorantly gathered, that the wicked fhall not rife in the flefh, to come and receiue Iudgement in the laft Day. Yea, with this opinion, was that learned Father, *Origen*, a while deluded. But, it is a great herefie: for, they fhall furely bee raifed, and fummoned

to

to that Doome (as appeareth in many places of holy Scripture) but there indeed, they fhal not be able to ftand out in their owne Iuftification, as belonging to the Affembly of the righteous. Becaufe, when they fhall thinke, to excufe themfelues ; the King fhall turne them forth, with this terrible fentence. *Goe, yee curfed, into euerlafting fire, which is prepared for the Deuill and his Angells.*

Matth. 25. 4L.

Obfer.   Hence then I obferue ; that there fhall bee a generall Doome, wherein both good and bad fhall be fummoned, before the Tribunall Seat of God. And that, althogh Hypocrites, like tares amongft wheat (or rather, like good wheat) may be fuffered, in this life, to fhrowd themfelues in the Church of God, and come into the Congregation of the Righteous, vnder the name of *Chriftians* : yet, in the harueft (that is) in this *Iudgment*; hee wlll feperate them. And the vngodly

godly ſhall not be able to *ſtand,* in
that Aſſembly of the Iuſt ; but *The* *Matth.* 13. 14.
Lord will gather the Righteous, which
are the wheat; *into his Granard* : *& caſt*
the ſinners, which are the chaffe ; *into*
vnquenchable fire.

But, that no weake conſcience may A Caueat.
be driuen into deſpaire. I deſire the
Reader, not to imagine, that euery
man, who hath the pollutions of ſin,
is in danger of this ſeparation ; for,
euery man is ſo guilty of ſinne, that
if God ſhould marke all that were a-
miſſe, and enter into Iudgements
with his ſeruants : None were able to
ſtand in the Iudgement. No, not the
moſt Righteous ; neither ſhould any
fleſh be ſaued in his ſight. We muſt Two ſorts of
then conſider, that there be two ſorts ſinnes.
of *Sinners.* The one regenerate, who
offends vnwillingly ; and falling into
tranſgreſſions , through infirmity,
by repentance, true contrition, and
amendment of life, riſeth againe ;
                                    and

and feekes forgiuenesse, in his Redeemer, *Iesus Chrift*. The other, vnregenerate; who, out of wicked impiety, and malicious wilfullnesse, followes without repentance, the ftudy and practice of finne; obftinately refufing, or neglecting the grace of *Chrift*, And they are fuch, whofe eftate is fo miferable, to be excluded, from the *Affembly of the Righteous*. The other, laying hold on *Chrift*, are by faith made righteous in him, and fhall be reckoned among the faithfull and happy Congregation.

Ver. 6.

    For, the LORD *knoweth the way of the righteous,* &c. The reafon is here giuen, why the Iuft man is fo much more happy, then the Sinner; and how it comes to paffe, that, *hee walketh not in the Counfells of the vngodly, nor ftandeth in the way of finners, nor fitteth in the feat of the fcornefull.* And why, in the laft Iudgement,

ment, there ſhall bee a ſeparation
made, and a difference put betweene
the good and the bad. And it is this,
God knoweth the way of the righteous.
and the way of the vngodly ſhall periſh.
Which implies, that there is a contra-
riety in their *way* ; and that therfore,
they cannot meet in one Congrega-
tion.

But why is it ſayd, *God knowes the*
way of the Righteous ? Doth hee not
alſo know the way of the wicked,
you will ſay? I anſwer, yes. For,
Gods diuine knowledge extends it
ſelfe to all. Yet, in this place, the
word, *knoweth,* includes, eſpecially, a
regard, or approbation ; and is, as if
he ſhould haue ſayd, God *acknowled-*
geth, takes care of, regards, or *allow-*
eth the way of the Righteous : and,
becauſe their endeauours and aimes
are, to ſhunne the Counſels of the
vngodly, and by obedient directing
themſelues, after the rule of the Sa-

I   cred

cred Word, to feeke his glory, with thofe *wayes*, that perifh not. Therefore, this God, of his free grace, keepeth them in the right path ; and by that direct courfe, conducteth them to the fame *bleffcdneffe*, whereunto hee foreknew it would lead them. And, that this word, *knoweth*, may be vnderftood, as is aforefayd,

Iob 9. 12.   to imply a *regard*, or *approbation*, ap-
Prou. 12. 10.   peareth in thefe enfuing places. *Pfal.* 101. 4. *Rom.* 8. 1. 5. 1. *Iohn* 3. 2. And fo much may be alfo prooued by that place of *Matthew*, where *Chrift* vfeth the contrary fpeech, to fhew the difrefpect that he would haue to the

Matth. 7. 23.   wicked. *I neuer knew you* (will he fay) *depart from me, yee workers of iniquity.* This word, *knoweth*, may haue refpect alfo to the fore-knowledge of their election. For (as fome vnderftand it) to that purpofe, S. *Paul* vfeth

2 *Tim.* 2. 19.   it in his fecond Epiftle to *Timothy*, chap. 2. and the 19. verfe. And writing

ting to the *Romans*, he ſaith. *Thoſe,* *Rom.* 8. 29.
whom he did foreknow, he did alſo pre-
deſtinate, to be conformed to the Image
of his Sonne.

But the way of the vngodly ſhall pe-
riſh. And that is; becauſe, God re-
gardeth not, neither is delighted with
their courſes. They propoſe vnto
themſelues a happineſſe; but come
ſhort of it: becauſe, their counſels,
endeauours, and all; are ouerthrown,
before they can attaine to the poſſeſ-
ſion therof. And needs muſt it be ſo.
Seeing it is, neither the right means,
which they vſe; nor, a true happi-
neſſe, which they ſeeke. For, wher-
to tends their ayme? Sure, not to
Gods glory; nor, to ſeeke their ſpiri-
tuall wel fare; nor any greater *bleſ-*
ſedneſſe, then the compaſſing, or en-
ioying of ſome brutiſh, or tranſitory
pleaſures. Which, before it be long,
either altogether faile them; or, in-
ſtead of a deſired happineſſe, are a

I 2   meanes,

meanes to bring vpon them the curfe of fome vnexpected miferie, which is euer the *period* of fuch *paths*. So, they at length, perceiue with much difcomfort, that their labors are loft, their time mif-fpent, & that (as the *Prophet* here faith) *Their way muft perifh*, and come to nought. In breefe then, I vnderftand thefe words, *The way of the vngodly fhall perifh :* As if the *Prophet* had fayd. The vngodly come fhort of bleffedneffe, and fhall be excluded from the Congregation of the Iuft ; becaufe, the Lord is re-gardleffe of them ; and fo, thofe vaine wayes and courfes, which they follow, fhall faile to bring them thither.

Obfer. 1.   Hence then, wee are taught, how to efteeme the world, with all thofe titles, honours, and fauours, where-withall fhee allureth us, to fetle our hearts, vpon the painted and vncer-taine felicities of this life : and to bee heed-

heedfull, that they draw vs not into
the way of deſtruction. And, as the
firſt part of the *Pſalme*, ought to win
vs, in reſpect of the felicitie, promi-
ſed to *the way of the Righteous:* ſo,
the ruine, that is heere threatned,
may terrifie vs from *the way of ſin-*
ners.

Further, wee may hence learne,   *Obſer.* 2.
not to bee deiected, in our miſeries,
though wee are mercileſly oppreſſed,
by our aduerſaries ; nor, be diſcom-
fited : becauſe the world neither pi-
ties, nor takes notice, of thoſe many
ſlanders, and ſecret iniuries, which
wee uniuſtly ſuffer. For, if God (as
it is here ſayd, hee doth) *knoweth,*
and regardeth, *the way of his* ſer-
uants, wee may be certaine, that he
ſeeth euery affliction in this iourney,
and will not leaue our oppreſſions
unreuenged.

We may alſo hence be taught ; not   *Obſer.* 2.
I 3   to

to take offence at the ſhort proſperi-
ty of the wicked ; nor, to bee allured
with the pleaſantneſſe of their waies.
For, though they bee delightfull to
the ſence, and goodly broad pathes ;
yet they lead to deſtruction, and, as
it is here told vs, they ſhall periſh.

Thus, according to my abilitie, I
haue gone thorow with an Expoſiti-
on vpon this *Pſalme.* Wherein,
though I haue followed no one ;
yet, I haue runne the ordinary way,
with other Expoſitors.   But, becauſe
I beleeue with S. *Auguſtine,* there is
no *Pſalme,* wherein the Author of
it, had no reſpect to *Chriſt.*   I will
ſhew you, how it may bee ſo aptly
applyed vnto him, as you ſhall eaſi-
ly beleeue ; that, although it may be
accommodated to all the Saints ;
yet, aboue others, the Bleſſed Man
(as we ſay) *per Antonomaſiam,* meanes
Chriſt ; and, that this *Pſalme,* was
principally intended of that *Iuſt One.*
For,

For, it is a *Song*, or *Pſalme*, wher-
in *bleſſedneſſe* is aſcribed, to that
thrice godly Man, who is no way
guilty of any kinde of ſinne ; whe-
ther it be of tranſgreſſion, omiſſion,
or originall. And who, but *He* only ;
(or thoſe, who haue receiued it by
Him) can be honoured with ſuch in-
nocency ; or capable of ſo high a dig-
nity, as this true *Bleſſedneſſe* : who a-
lone, perfeⅽtly fufilled the Law ? And
was obedient, euen to the death ?
Doubtleſſe, none. For, all that are
ſo called, are ſo entitled by him.
And hee, is that for-euer-bleſſed
Man, whoſe foot *neuer walkt*, in the
crooked *way of the vngodly* ; nor,
ſtood in the *ſlippery path of ſinners.*

He it was, who in true humilitie,
taught the ſimple truth ; and negle-
ⅽting the vain dignities of the world,
neuer repoſed himſelfe, in the impe-
rious *ſeat of the Scornfull*, whith the

I 4   diſdaindifdainfull *Pharifies*. He it is, whofe delight is in fulfilling the Will and *Law* of his *Father*; and in the accomplifhment therof, hee ferioufly exercifed himfelfe, both *day & night*. He, is that flourifhing *Tree, planted by the pure riuers, of water of life*; *cleere as cryftall, and proceeding from the Throne of God*: euen that Tree, which is planted in the middeft of new *Ieru-falem*, and hath brought forth the fruit of our faluation, in *due feafon*, and in the fulneffe of time: according to the Scriptures.

This is he, *whofe leafe fhall not fall.* That is; his words fhall not fall to the ground, but remaine euer flourifhing, and ferue to heale the *Nations*; according to the Prophecy of Saint *Iohn*. And doubtleffe, *whatfoeuer he doth fhall profper.* But the wicked are not fo: that is; the *Iewes* and other wicked perfecutors of Chrift;

Reuel. 22.

Chriſt; with ſuch as by Faith, put
not on his righteouſneſſe ; are in a
quite contrary eſtate. Like *Chaffe
ſcattered with the wind* ; yea, in a miſe-
rable, vaine, and vnſetled condition.
And therefore, when this our redee-
mer ſhall enter into *Iudgement* with
the world ; ſuch an *Antipathie* will
be betweene him, and vnrighteouſ-
neſſe ; as they ſhall not be able *to
ſtand* before him. But, when the
Children of his kingdome ſhall be
congregated at his right hand, to
partake with him in eternall bliſſe ;
as they haue beene partakers with
him, in his graces here : then ſhall
the wicked be ſhut out of their aſ-
ſemblies ; to be caſt into eternall per-
dition. And of this ſeparation, the
reaſon is ; becauſe the *Righteous* doe
follow *Chriſt* in the *way* of his *Goſ-
pel*; and walke in the *Faith* which
he hath approued. Whilſt the *Iewes*,
and

and ſuch as are without the *Church:*
ſecking ſaluation by the workes of
the *Law,* or following ſome ſuch
wrong, or by paths; thcir *way* failes
them, and comes vnto an cnd, when
it hath brought them to the left
hand of the Iudge. Where;
they arc fartheſt off
from *Bleſſed-*
neſſe.

Medi-

Meditations, vpon the firſt
PSALME; in verſe.

The Contents of theſe Meditations.

The Muſe, firſt ſings the heauenly Bliſſe;
  and ſhewes how vaine the earthly is.
The wrong way thither, with the right:
  are here, laid open to your ſight.
The iuſt mans, glorious weal it ſhowes.
  the ſinners, matchleſſe, endleſſe woes.
And good, and bad, are both expreſt;
  that you may learne, and chuſe the beſt.

Y Ou; *whoſe ore-weary, reſtleſſe ſoules deſire;*
  The prime content, to which all creatures tend;
                                            And

And to that matchleffe Bleffedneffe *afpire:*
Which (though moft fceke) moft faile of in the end.

Lo; here a heauenly Mufe *points out the* way,
Wherein you fafe may runne, and neuer more
In thofe blinde-crooked paths of danger ftray;
Which haue mifled fo many heretofore.

No prize *vnfought, or trifling newes fhe fings;*
But that, for which your many adventures are:
That, which to gaine; Rich, *poore-men flaues &* Kings,
doe howerly, watch and labour, fweat and warre.

Yet moft perhaps in vaine; For, what they get
By their endeauour in the Common Courfe
Yeeldes no felicities but Counterfeit:
And often, driues them on, from bad, to worfe.

Yong bloods, are fnared with the painted fweetes
Of luft, or beauty: and beleeue that there,
Is full contentment. The rich glutton greetes
His boundleffe appetite, with curious fare.

The worldling, makes inqueft for happineffe;
And dreames, to finde it in a trade of gaine:
He in his Auarice *himfelfe doth bleffe,*
And as his thirft is, fuch his bliffe *doth faine.*

The happineffe *of fome, in rich attire,*
High Titles, or vaine-glorious pompe depends;

A

A louing wife, another doth deſire:
Good-toward Children, or vnfained friends.
   Kings, in their awfull thrones of Soueraignty;
And vncontrould prerogatiues delight:
The Courtier, ſooths vp them in vanitie;
And thinkes it heauen, to be their Fauourite.
   But they are all deceiu'd; For, all theſe be
Vaine-fruitleſſe aymes; like graſſe will beauty fade,
Luſt, will to loathing turne, and then ſhall he
Who there ſought happineſſe, be haples made.
   A hungry famine, may thoſe Creatures waſt
Which glut cram'd Epicures: or ſome diſeaſe,
May take away the pleaſure of the taſt.
And where is then, the happineſſe of theſe?
   Fire; water, theeues or Ruſt, conſume the ſtore
Of richeſt men; and he, that but to day
Had great poſſeſſions, is to morrow poore:
Or dies; or ſees it, to his foes a pray.
   Gay cloathes, to Rags we haue exchanged ſeene.
Foule ſtinch, and wormes the proudeſt ruin'd haue.
And thoſe; that dearer than their ſoules haue beene,
Haue ſhar'd their wealth, & laught thē to their graue
   She; that hath kiſt, embrac't and ſworne to-day
A Thouſand vowes of kindeueſſe in thine arme:
                   When

When thou art cold, and in a fheete of clay;
Shall keepe anothers bed and bofome warme.
   Thofe Princes, that have largeft kingdomes got,
Are neuer quiet, whilft there doe remaine
Some other Emperies which they haue not:
Nay, if they might, the next, and next obtaine
   Till they had all.   Perhaps they would be fad
(If not for fome poore toy or Humor croft)   (had:
That more things were not knowne which might be
Or left, what they enioyed fhould be loft.
   What bliffe affords a Crowne; when treafons, war,
And nightly cares, difturbes the owners reft?
More fad amid their armed troopes they are,
Then he that walkes alone with naked breft.
   Though all the meanes, to be fecure they take
Some horror, ftill appeares their foules to grieue;
And greatneffe, neuer fuch a guard could make,
But forrowes would get in, and aske no leaue.
   Though, they had all the pleafures of the fence,
And ten times doubled their prerogatiue;
Though Parafites applaude their Excellence,
And yeelde them adoration while they liue:
   Though they attained to as much, as he
Who on the Iewifh Throne next Dauid fate:

Had

Had ſo much wiſedome, and could prying be
Through every Creature, to behold their ſtate.
    When that were done ; but little hope had they
From any thing on earth, content to gather.
That great wiſe Prince, made tryall ; and could ſay :
That, to the ſoule they brought vexation rather.

    And, when pale death aſſailes ; the thoughts & feare
Which trouble pooreſt men : ſhall ceaze their ſoule.
Their paines, ſhall be as ſharpe as Bond mens are ;
Their fleſh ſhall ſtinke as much ; and be as foule.

    Yea, er'e their breath forſake them one whole houre,
Their greateſt glorie, may be turn'd to ſcorne ;
But in one Age, the Rumor of their power
May be no more then his, that is vnborne.

    And then ; alas ! to what poore fortunes brought
Are thoſe ; whoſe bliſſe, on will of theſe, depends ?
Such ; as nor do, nor ſpeake, nor ſcarce thinke ought ;
But that, which to their Princes humor tends ?

    For theſe ; are Honours tennants but at will ;
Which when he liſt, the giuer may recall :
And cauſeleſſe (if he pleaſe) obieſt ſome ill ;
To iuſtifie his dealing, with their fall.

    And what a miſerable ſtate were this,
For any, to be deemed happy in ?

                                        Poore

Poore foules awake ; fee ; fee what truft there is
In that, wherewith you haue deluded beene.
  Let wantons, *feeke in luft what is not there.*
Let Epicures, *at Feafts for bliffe enquire.*
Let Mifers *looke on duft, till duft they are :*
And worldly men, *the worlds vaine loue defire.*
  Let Kings *of Earth* ; *affect an earthly Crowne.*
Let Courtiers *at the Court attend their Fates.*
And whilft they catch the bubbles of renowne ;
Let fooles ; *ftill wonder, at their happy ftates.*
  But you ; *that haue the end of thefe, defcernd,*
And furer grounds of bleffedneffe would know :
Come, heare what of a Prophet, *I haue learn'd* :
Who, fung this heauenly fubiect, long agoe.
  He taught my Mufe ; *and you, fhe teacheth how,*
Beft beauties, beft perfection to imbrace.
With Angels foode, fhe will replenifh you ;
And make you richer, then old Adam *was.*
  In ftead of mens falfe friendfhips, and their loue
Vnperfect, and inconftant, here below :
You, fhall be deere vnto the Saints *aboue,*
And into fellowfhip with Angels *grow.*
  Where you fhall loue, and be belou'd of all ;
Without (the leaft) diftruft, or Ieloufie :

                                        And

And death, or time, of nought depriue you ſhall;
But yeeld content (at full) eternally.
 If, with your vanities, you can diſpence,
And ſlight thoſe fauors, which each worldling craues;
You ſhall be Fauorites, to that great Prince,
To whom, Earths greateſt Monarks are but ſlaues.
 Such wiſhed honours, She ſhall bring you to,
As Kings can neither giue; not take away.
And, that you may not feare, what fleſh can do,
Shall be as free; and full as great as they.
 Yea, that true Bliſſe, to which all writings tend;
And moſt are yet to learne: here, know you ſhall.
By knowing, may enioy it in the end;
Enioying be contented there withall:
Vntill your ſoules, enriched with that ſtore,
Shall neuer know deſire, or lothing more.
 But, you muſt liſten with attention then;
And hitherto, your vtmoſt power enforce:
For, 'tis not; 'tis not (oh you ſonnes of men)
Obtain'd, by euery ordinary courſe.
 The way to bliſſe; is neither made by ſtrength,
Nor humane policie. Though many a traƐt,
Makes ſhew of leading thither; yet, at length,
It turnes another way, and brings to wrack.

K

The

The Pagans, *had a thought, some* God-head *should*
Direct them thither ; and in feare they might,
Misse that good Deity, *which guide them could :*
They seru'd too many Gods, *and lost it quite.*

The old Philosophers (*not knowing this ;*
That Nature, *by our fall, was growne corrupt*)
By Morall Vertues, *onely sought for blisse :*
Which did, their hoped Passage, interrupt.

For, when they had done all, which might be
By strict Morality, *to gaine their passe ;* (*wrought,*
And time, their course, vnto an end had brought,
Their ayme they mist ; because, Christ *wanting was.*

For, though some good they did ; yet, missing him,
To sanctisie their vertues, and to take
Those faults away, which had escaped them :
Into this rest, no entrance could they make.

The blinded Iewes, *by ceremonious lawes,*
And strict obseruing of their ancient guise,
Haue labour'd for it ; but, vpon some cause,
That way was long since chang'd, and from-ward lies
By vaine will-worship others goe. And some,
By formall shewes, of zealous sanctitie.
By way of their owne merits, many come :
And come farre short, of true felicitie.

A thou-

A thouſand other, crooked paths there be ;
Which ſeeme, to be direct ; yet, lead aſtray :
Leſt therefore, ſome of thoſe, miſcarry thee,
That haſt a longing, to the bleſſed way ;
 Who happy are ; lo, here it ſhall be ſhowne,
 And how, thou mayſt thy ſelfe, be ſuch an one.

VERS. I.

Bleſſed is the man, that doth not walke in the counſell of the vngodly, nor ſtand in the way of ſinners, nor ſit in the ſeat of the ſcornfull.

Firſt, *get thee out of that vngodly* way,
 (The way of Nature) *in which, all the race*
Of Adams *Progeny ; haue gone aſtray.*
Walke out of it, into the way of Grace.
 To which, there lyeth no hard paſſage, thence :
For, if thou wade, but thorow Baptiſmes *ford,*
And paſſe the thorny hedge, of Penitence *:*
Thou ſtraight art guided thither, by the Word.

    K 2   *Yet,*

Yet, take thou heede, when thus thou entred art ;
Lest that corruption, which doth still remaine :
By vaine affections, ill-aduise the heart,
To walke *with the* vngodly, *backe againe.*

Cast not thine eyes about, on those gay bayts ;
That grow, beside the way of Blessednesse :
But, shun thou all occasion, that awayts,
To draw thee into paths of wickednesse.

Let not the loue of honour, pleasure, ease,
Reuenge, lust, enuy, pride, *or* auarice :
Nor any such ill Counsellours, *as these ;*
Thy feet, vnto an euill course entice.

Pursue not worldly things, as worldly men,
That know not God, or true religion, do :
But, giue his Honour first respect ; and then,
With moderation, seeke the creature to.

Let no desire, without that compasse stray ;
Which honesty and piety hath set.
For, if thy thoughts doe euer breake away,
And Counsels *of vngodly longings get.*

They will not leaue thee ; but, from lust, to lust,
Allure thee on, in the vngodly path :
Vntill, they bring thee, to some act vniust.
And there, the sinners way *beginning hath.*

                                              Oh !

Oh! if through weakneſſe, and attending to
Vngodly Counſels; *thou ſhalt thither rome:*
As all indeede (though all their beſt they doe)
Into the way, of euill doers, come.

    Yet, ſtand *not there; continue not in ſin:*
But, by repentance, ſoone returne againe:
Leſt, thou ſhouldſt, by inſiſting long therin;
Affect it, and for euer there remaine.

    Vſe, gets a habit; and the habit got,
The title of a Sinner, gaineth thee:
And ſin, in this gradation reſteth not,
Till to a Scorner, thy Commencement bee.

    And then beware. For, if degree thou take
So far; and be a Doctor of their Chaire:
The next progreſſion, thou from thence canſt make;
Is either hell immediate or diſpaire.

    In thinking ill; we doe from heauen-ward goe;
In acting it, we further run aſtray:
But, if we to deride religion grow;
There's hardly hope, that we repent vs may.

    For, though God can the courſe of nature turne;
Bid aire deſcend, and earth aboue it riſe:
Quench heat in fire, make frozen water burne;
And in all creatures, change the qualities.

            K 3   Yet,

 Yet, that he therfore will; *it followes not,*
And ſo; *although he can repentance giue,*
To ſuch, as haue a wicked habit got:
And, in deſpight of him and vertue liue.

 Aſſoone, ſhall I beleeue; *that deſperate Churle,*
Who, from a rough ſteep cliffe, or high Tower wall,
Himſelf a furlong from the top doth hurle;
May raiſe himſelfe, in middeſt of the fall:

 As that; *the* Sinner, *who, of wilfullneſſe,*
Hath caſt himſelfe downe, from the hold of grace;
Can leaue that deep-deep gulf of wickedneſſe,
And in the rocke of mercy, get a place.

 It is a rare gain'd fauour, *when God daignes*
That vicious liuer grace, at his laſt breath:
Who, from no ſinne, for loue of Good, refraines;
Nor, thinkes to aske forgiueneſſe, vntill death.

 But, 'tis a Miracle, *if euer hee*
Shall, in his life, or death, forgiueneſſe get;
Who knowes, and ſcornes, the means that profer'd be:
For, neuer was it found exampled yet.

 Of theſe three ſteps; *oh! be yee wary then*;
To ſit, *or* ſtande, *or* walke, *doe you forbeare*:
In feat, *or* way, *or* counſell, *with thoſe men*;
That Scorners, Sinners, *or* Vngodly *are.*

                     Nor,

Nor, will this be enough. For, as the Swaine,
Who ſitteth downe, when he himſelfe hath loſt :
Is no more like, to reach his home againe ;
Then he, that quite another way doth poſt.

   So they, who thinke it is enough, to ſhun
The ordinary path, that Sinners *tread ;*
And take no heed, what good is to be done :
Shall neuer, of true happineſſe be ſped.

   Or, like as they ; who, without Sterne or Card,
Dare ſeeke an vnknowne Coaſt, for golden ore :
May crowne their voyage, with a rich reward ;
Aſſoone as thoſe, that vſe nor Saile, nor Oare.

   Right ſo ; as well may ſuch, as looſely liue,
The prize of happineſe attaine vnto :
As thoſe ; who hope, they ſhall at bliſſe ariue,
Although not one foot thither-ward, they goe.

   And therfore liſten, my aduiſe vnto :
That you may learne, what you haue yet, to doe.

K 4   VERS.

VERS. 2.

But his delight is in the Law of the
LORD, and in his Law doth he
meditate day and night.

(hath ;

WHen *Gods great mercy, safely brought thee*
From all the counsels, waies, & seats *of sin :*
Lest thou stray backe againe ; take vp the path
That iust against it lies ; and walke therin.
   Keepe on foreright ; let nothing tarry thee :
For, non-progression, *there ; regression is.*
But, if thou in continuall motion bee ;
(Though flow it doth appeare) it brings to blisse.
   To helpe thee on, two sacred Scrowles *there are ;*
Which may direct thy Pilgrimage *throughout :*
They profer'd are, to euery Passenger ;
And can informe them, where they stand in doubt.
   The first sure marke, *that tels vs we are right,*
In this blest progresse, and haue quite abhord
The way of Sinners ; is a true delight,
Vnto the Law, *of our* eternall LORD.

Whilst

Whilſt that affection holds ; there is no feare,
Or danger of relapſe. No wicked traine,
Which the vngodly roundeth in thine eare,
Can moue thee, to partake therein againe.

   But, leſt thy heart deceiue thee (for mans heart
Is falſe, and oft betrayes him to his foe)
Make triall of his truth (if wiſe thou art)
And I will ſhew thee, how thou mayſt doe ſo.

   Search, if there be no carnall vaine reſpect,
That drawes on this delight ; or, if to thee
Thoſe volumes, which thou ſeemeſt to affect :
Be pleaſing, as the Word of God they bee.

   Try, if thy Conſcience, will for witneſſe come,
That thou haſt, with a true endeavour, ſought
To exerciſe his Law ; abroad, at home,
By day, by night, in deed, in word, in thought.

   For, know well this, that by the Night and Day,
It is not onely meant, in weale and woe :
Or, that thou ſhouldſt, from time to time aſſay,
Vntired, in the way of Bliſſe to goe.

   But, thou with knowledge, muſt proceed therin.
By pondering Gods Law, both in the Night,
Of his Old Teſtament, which veyl'd it in :
And in the New ; that Day-like gaue it light.

                       Firſt,

First, thou must meditate, how man was made,
And (being made) a Law from God receiu'd :
How he transgrest, and fell ; and falling, had
That Law *(with some new circumstance) reuiu'd.*

Thou must consider, how the same was writ,
First, in the heart *by* nature ; *then in* ftone :
And how, in Effence, *neuer altring it.*
Of Accidents, *God added many a one.*

Thou must conceiue ; the prime Effentiall part
Of this great Law, *was* Chrift : *and* Chrift, *the End*
Of all those things, which thou inform'd of art ;
Throughout the booke, *before his comming pend.*

Thou must obserue, how euery passage there,
Doth shadow out that substance ; and foretell,
In holy riddles, what did plaine appeare ;
When his, so long-expected Day *befell.*

Then, hauing passed o're the cloudy Night,
Of Types, *darke* Figures, *hidden* Prophesies,
And deepe Ænigma's; *thou must seeke the light,*
To be instructed in these Mysteries.

Thou, in the Day, *Gods* Law *must meditate.*
The Day *of his* New Teftament ; *wherein,*
The Morning-Star *appear'd : and set a date,*
To that thicke darkneffe, which so long had bin.

And,

And, when thou ſeeſt how all the viſions, dreams,
And Propheſies *obſcure, diſcouered are* ;
By thoſe bright-ſhining, and thrice-glorious beames,
Which, at thy Saviours *comming did appeare.*

Thou muſt (in that faire ſun-ſhine of his grace)
Conſider, with what infinite reſpect,
God daign'd to pity, thy diſtreſſed caſe :
And how much, Hee, thy well fare did affect.

From poynt, to poynt, thou well conſider muſt ;
The Law *in his* New Teſtament *declar'd,*
The Law *of* Faith, *which makes the ſinner iuſt :*
And opes the gate, which Adams *crime had barr'd.*

Theron affix thy heart ; *and learne to know,*
How God, from age to age, this Law *deriu'd.*
How, that of Moſes, *did aboliſht grow :*
With, what muſt be perform'd ; *and what beleeu'd.*

For, thoſe who thus much learne ; *& teach, & then*
Continue practiſe, in a courſe vpright :
May beſt enſtiled be, thoſe happy men ;
That meditate Gods Law, both Day and Night.

If this thou reach ; *or, but endeauor well,*
To that degree of Grace, *which God ſhall daine :*
The Worthies of the world, thou ſhalt excell ;
And win the prize, for which they ſeeke in vaine.

                                        Yea ;

Yea ; cheare thy ſoule ; and let nor paine, nor care,
Nor loſſe, nor height, nor depth, nor ought at all,
The world can tell thee ; make thy ſoule to feare ;
For this ; to Bleſſedneſſe, *conduct thee ſhall.*

   Nay, thou already, therein ; bleſſed art.
And euen, thoſe ſtormes of troubles, that oppreſſe,
and hem thee round about, on euery part ;
Shall make more perfect, thy true happineſſe.

   Which will be ſuch ; as tongue-tide eloquence,
Shall be vnable to report thy bliſſe :
Yea, ſo vnthought of, is that excellence,
No heart, e're halfe imagin'd, what it is.

   And, ah ! what pleaſures can be more excelling ;
   Then thoſe, that are beyond both thought & telling?

VERS. 3.

And he, ſhall be like a Tree planted
   by the riuers of waters, that will
   bring forth his fruit in ſeaſon,
   his leafe ſhall not fade, and what-
   foeuer he doth, ſhall proſper.

But

BVt, ſenſuall men, muſt haue a ſenſuall touch,
Of what we tell them ; and ſome obiects view :
By which, their reaſon, may perceiue as much,
As, either words, or ſignes, haue power to ſhew.

For els, although the portion be but ſmall,
Which they (at beſt) of theſe things can conceiue ;
That little portion will be nought at all.
And (as in vaine) our labour we may leaue.

That (therfore) you, ſome little glympſe may ſee,
Of that abundance of contentment ; which
Muſt wait on thoſe, that this way happy bee :
And make them, without want, or loathing, rich.

Marke well, thoſe euer-green-leafe-bearing Trees ;
Which, in ſome fruitfull valley planted are :
Where ; with their nature, ſoyle, and clime agrees ;
And riuers flow, to moyſt them, all the yeare.

Where, neither Summers heat, nor Winters cold,
Nor ſterrile drought, nor rotting wet, offends.
But where, the aire doth ſuch good temper hold,
That floures doe leaues, and fruits ſtill floures attend.

For, as thoſe trees, may ſo much moyſture take,
As they ſhall either neede, or can containe ;
And nothing miſſe of, which compleat may make,
What to a trees well-being, doth pertaine.

So ;

So, *by the loue of Gods* eternall law ;
Men soules, are set anew in Paradise.
Where ; *from the* Riuers *of Gods grace, they draw*
The nourishments, of true felicities.

Their state is constant, lasting euermore.
And not one true contentment, can be found,
In Earth, or heauens immesurable store ;
But, with that wisht perfection they are Crown'd.

Their soules haue all that full of happinesse,
Which can in any soule, contained be :
As trees, best planted ; *haue that fruitfulnesse,*
Which most becomes the nature of a Tree.

They in the Church, *Gods Garden planted are* ;
Where Christ, *that liuing rock, remaineth still.*
And, from his side (the crimson Fountaine there)
Lifes pretious liquors, plentiously distill.

His blessed Sacraments *and faithfull* Word,
Preserues their growth, and makes them fructifie ;
Till they, doe fruit for euery Moneth afford,
And beare the leaues, of blest eternity.

Neuer ; *no neuer, can their beauty fall*
from ripe perfection ; *but, as you haue seene*
A goodly bay-tree flourish : *So, they shall*
Be, winter, sommer, spring and Autumne greene.

And

And then ; in all things, they ſhall proſper too ;
What er'e betide them ; or what ere they do.

VERS. 4.

The vngodly *are* not ſo : but
are like the chaffe which the
winde driueth away.

BVt, leſt that all which hath been ſaid ſhould faile
To make you well conceiue, how much it may
Redound to euery ſeuerall mans availe ;
To grow approued, in this bleſſed way.
  And ſince, the natures of moſt men, are ſuch ;
As that, the promiſes of beſt contents,
Do ſeldome halfe preuaile with them ſo much,
As ſlauiſh feare, of threatned puniſhments.
  Know this ; that whatſoeuer mortall wight,
The way of life, here taught him, doth refuſe :
He ſhall not onely, be depriued quite,
Of theſe ; and all thoſe hopes, that he purſues.
  But, his condition, from the bleſſed, ſhall
So farre be differing ; that, no ſtrife, vnreſt,

Shame,

Shame, horror, or misfortune, can befall :
But, his dispairing soule, it shall arrest.

  If you e're noted haue, how far we prize
The lightest chaffe, beneath the waighty graine ;
How safe the one is kept, how firme it lies ;
How vile we count the other, and how vaine.

  Betwixt the worldling, and right-blessed man ;
Such difference is there. For, as euery winde,
The sleighted chaffe, doth this, and that way fan :
And no abiding place, will let it finde.

  So, that vngodly, irreligious crue,
Who make their heauen on earth ; and scorning these
True paths of blessednesse, those toyes pursue,
Which may their owne proud eye, or belly please :

  Eu'n those ; by puffes of windy vanity,
Strong-raging passion, and vntamed lust :
Are hurried, with such strange incertainty,
To this, and that, euery act vniust.

  As, whatsoeuer rest they seeme to take,
Their life is wholly restlesse ; and no day,
No houre, no minute, sleeping, or awake :
In any setled peace, continue they.

  The Glutton *would be rich ; but is perplext,
To thinke, that he must then abate his fare.*

The

The Miſer, *would haue honour ; and is vext,*
To ſee how coſtly, courts and greatneſſe are.

   Th' Ambitious, *couets eaſe ; but findes it mars*
His high deſignes : and may his hopes deface.
The Coward, *would haue fame ; but feares the wars :*
And Leachers, *doubt diſeaſes, or diſgrace.*

   Yea, in their hearts, ſo many ſtrange deſires,
Are often lodg'd, and thoſe ſo oppoſite :
That, by enioying what one luſt requires,
They bar themſelues, ſome other wiſht delight.

   But grant, their outward ſtate were ſetled more,
More thriuing, and in loſſe, and changes leſſe :
That they haue eaſe, and honour, with their ſtore ;
And to the world-ward, ſetled happineſſe.

   Yet, neither can they wake, nor ſleep in peace.
Their conſcience, like a flaming-fire within ;
Will ſeare, and ſcorch, and burne : and never ceaſe
Vntill diſpaire, *to neſtle there begin.*

   Or ſay they ſcape this to.   And whilſt they liue,
So ſtupid grow, that in ſecuritie,
They ſenſeleſſe lie ; vntill their ſoules, it driue
Into a helpleſſe, helliſh lethargie.

   Yet, which is worſe ; far worſe, then what is paſt :
(And makes me tremble, when I call to minde

L

Their

Their fearfull caufe) there is a Day *at laft*;
In which they pay for all, that is behinde.
　　But, thofe fad terrours will my Mufe *rehearfe,*
　　In what fhe fingeth, on the following Verfe.

Vers. 5.

Therefore the Vngodly fhall not
ftand in the Iudgement, nor Sin-
ners in the Congregation of the
Righteous.

OH *you! whom neither Gods eternall loue,*
　　Nor vertues beauty, nor his facred Law;
Nor promifes of matchleffe Bliffe, *can moue:*
Nor threatned loffe therof, preferue in awe.
　　You; *that are neither wooed to repent,*
　　Your follies, for this lifes vncertainties:
Nor won, to feeke the way of true content;
By inward feares, nor outward miferies.
　　Though none of thefe, can gaine you to affay,
For that high Bleffedneffe, *which crownes the good*;
　　　　　　　　　　　　　　　　　Nor,

Nor force you, to forgoe that damned way,
Which ſeemeth pleaſing, vnto fleſh and blood.

  Oh yet ! for that rare priuiledge, which thoſe,
Who loue Gods Law, ſhall haue ; when flaming fire,
Doth all this maſſie Globe of earth encloſe :
To rectifie your courſe, I you require.

  For know ; there are not onely, in this world,
A thouſand miſcheefes, plagues, heart-ſtinging cares,
And dreadfull Iudgements ; ready to be hurld,
From Heauens high Battlements, about your eares :
  But, after death, there is a time will come,
To haſten all, which is delayed here.
A Day *of vengeance, and a* Day *of Doome :*
In which ; all Adams *Of-ſpring, ſhall appeare.*

  The dreadfull Iudge, *in glory will deſcend ;*
With his great Hoſt of Heauen, compaſt round.
Seas, Earth, and Hell, ſhall at his Bar attend,
With al their priſoners, when the Trump *doth ſound.*

  A hideous Bonefire, through the world ſhall blaze.
The Roofe of Heauen, ſhall like a parchment ſcrowle,
At his appearing, ſhrinke ; and with amaze,
The dead ſhall riſe ; the liuing, frighted howle.

  And, neither ſex, condition, nor degree ;
Shall haue reſpect, or place : but every one,

L 2

Without

Without diſtinction, ſhall in perſon bee;
Before the great Almighties *Iudgement Throne.*
    Your pureſt beauties, ſhall attraƐ no more,
That Iudges *eye; then fouleſt vlcers can.*
He, *ſhall not bribed be, with* Indian *Ore:*
Nor moued, by the flattring tongue of man.

    Kings, *are in his eſtecme no more that* Day,
Then ſlaues: or, pooreſt wretches on the earth.
He, *prizeth no man, for his rich aray:*
Nor ought regardeth, nobleneſſe of birth.

    In his Grand Court *of Iuſtice; he admits,*
No ſubtill Trauers, *no* Demurs, Repeales,
Delayes, Iniunƈtions, *neither any* Writs
Of Error, *nor* Excuſes, *nor* Appeales.

    No bribed Fauorites, *hath* Hee *to raiſe,*
By motions at his Bar: *On him, attends*   *(ſwayes:*
No Groomes, *nor* Kinſmen, *that his* Lordſhip
To wreſt the courſe of Iuſtice, to their ends.

    No great man *ſends his letters to entreat,*
To change his ſentence; nor a coſtly fee:
That hires him any way to mitigate,
What he hath once, reſolued to decree.

    You ſons of Adam; *you ſhall doubtleſſe come,*
(Though ſleight perhaps my counſell may appeare.

                               To

To ſuch a Iudge ; *to ſuch impartiall Doome* :
And finde all true, that I foretell you here.

  Yea ; *if you hearken not to the command*
Of your Creator ; *nor, his* Law *delight* :
You ſhall not in that Iudgement *guiltleſſe ſtand.*
But fall condemned, in the Iudges *ſight.*

  And, when the Righteous, *are aſſembled there* :
With, Come you Bleſſed. *And at full poſſeſſe,*
(According to the promiſe, made them here)
The ioyfull Crowne of endleſſe happineſſe.

  Then, with a curſe *excluded, ſhall you goe* ;
Amongſt the damned ſpirits, into hell :
Shut out from bliſſe, *into a world of woe* ;
Amid thoſe tortures, which no tongue can tell.

  And when, as many hundred thouſand yeares,
You haue endur'd ; *as there be on the ſhore,*
Small ſtones, or ſands : *the time no ſhorter weares* ;
Nor will your plagues grow fewer, then before.

  Nay, though you were reſeru'd for no more paine,
Nor other diſcontentment, then the miſſe,
Of that great good, to which the iuſt attaine :
In (ſuch priuation) hell enough there is.

  We ſee, that when ambitious *men haue got*
Reſpect, and meanes enough, to liue at reſt :

L 3

Yet,

Yet, if they miſſe ſome marke, wherat they ſhot;
They fret, as men without compare vnbleſt.

   We ſee that Worldlings; *who, on tempting gold,*
Haue ſet their thoughts, can ten times better beare
The brunt of labour; hunger, thirſt and cold:
Then liue well fed, and warme; with coffers bare.

   We likewiſe know; that Louers, *barr'd the ſight*
Of their deare Miſtreſſes; *can ne're receiue*
Content; nor cauſe of comfort, or delight:
Though free from outward paines, or want, they liue.

   Nay rather; it torments, and greeueth more
Their vexed ſoules, then ſmart of body may:
And more, themſelues, they thinke inſulted ore;
Then if, for triall, on the Racke they lay.

   This we haue knowne. And if, priuation can
On earth ſo torture; where euen torments are
Imperfect. Oh! how much more greeuous than,
Shall thoſe ſoules finde it, that muſt feele it there?

   If here; thou canſt not brooke contempt, diſgrace;
To be depriu'd of honour, or the view
Of thoſe falſe beauties; wherein thou do'ſt place
Contentment here. Ah! what will there enſue?

   How? how, wilt thou endure it, wretched Elfe?
When thou ſhalt know, what riches they poſſeſſe,

Who

Who ſhall be bleſſed : and perceiue thy ſelfe
Debarr'd, for euer, of that happineſſe ?
   When thou eternally, ſhalt be a ſcorne ;
Of thy contentment ſtript ; of peace, of friends :
Of all the fellowſhip of Saints, forlorne ;
And no Companions left, but damned Fiends.
   When thou ; to endleſſe darkneſſe baniſhed,
Shalt burne with the deſire, of ſeeing Him.
With whoſe perfections, Angels *eyes are fed ;*
And in reſpect of whom, the Sun is dim ?
   Oh ! what a paſſion will torment thy ſoule ;
When thou ſhalt miſſe that ſweetneſſe ? And imbrace,
Inſteed therof ; deformity, as foule,
As hell, can put vpon her lothſome face.
   What wilt thou doe, alas ! when thou muſt beare
All this great horror ; and ſharp pangs withall ?
For thus ; euen thus, will the vngodly fare :
When that great Iudgement, *ouertake them ſhall.*
   And it ſhall adde, vnto their torment to ;
   What e're they ſuffer, ſay, or thinke, or do.

       L 4   VERS.

VERS. 6.

For, the LORD knoweth the
way of the Righteous : but the
way of the Vngodly fhall pe-
rifh.

BVt that *no* righteous *Man, deterr'd may be,*
From labouring, for his Bleffedneffe, *through*
That the Almighty, *doth nor mark, nor fee* : *(doubt,*
How many painfull fteps, he paceth out.
   And likewife, that no Sinner *may, vnwarned,*
His owne vaine way purfue, with falfe furmize :
That God doth ouer-paffe, as vndifcerned ;
The courfe he takes ; *or winke at villanies.*
   Know this, you happy men, that would attaine
To perfect Bliffe. *That, howfoe're you feeme*
Obfcur'd on earth ; *and oft to fpend in vaine,*
Your labours, and your liues, without efteeme.
   There's not a drop of bloud, a figh, a teare,
An inward fmarting, or an outward grone.

A

A ſleight vnkindneſſe, or a ſcoffe you beare :
But the Almighty *knowes them, every one.*
    If you but ſweat a little, in this path :
He ſees it ; and in time, reward it will.
Not one ſad thought, your heart in ſecret hath :
But God both knowes *therof, and mindes it ſtill.*

    Though you cloſe priſoners were, in ſtricteſt thrall,
Neglected of the world, and ſeene by none,
But ſuch oppreſſours, as would ſmother all,
Which for your praiſe, or comfort, might bee knowne.

    Though you were mew'd, where none might come to
What you haue done, or ſuffer'd, in this way : (tell,
And being in ſome dungeon, forc'd to dwell ;
Had mourn'd, to death, ſhut from the ſight of day.

    Yea, though your foes ſhould labour, to obſcure
Your good endeavours, with a ſlanderous fame ;
And brand you, with vile actions ſo impure,
That all men thought you, worthy death and ſhame.

    Yet, God ; *whoſe bright, and all beholding eyes,*
Viewes preſent, paſt, and euery future thing :
Sees vndeceiu'd ; and whatſoe're he ſpies,
To light, will one day, to your glory bring.
He knowes ; & knowing, doth approue your courſe.
And what he doth approue, ſhall neuer faile.

                                            Nor

Nor Man, nor Deuill ; policie, nor force :
Againſt his power, or knowledge, can preuaile.

   Oh therfore ! droop not, though a thouſand ſtormes,
Or likelyhoods of ruine, may appeare :
For, when diſpaire puts on her vglieſt forme ;
Then ; is your moſt aſſured ſafety neere.

   Nor boaſt, you Sinners ; as if you had found
A readier courſe, vnto the trueſt bliſſe,
Then righteous men ; becauſe, your way is crown'd
With more vaine honour, then their labour is.

   Nor, let your painted pleaſures, gull you ſo ;
To make you dreame, that God deceiu'd will bee.
Or, that an vnſuſpeéted courſe you go :
Becauſe, the world your danger cannot ſee.

   For, though a while you proſper, and delude
With ſhewes of happineſſe, the blinded eye
Of fooles ; and the abuſed multitude,
That are in loue, with your gay vanity.

   Yet ; ruine, ſhame, and deſolation ſhall
Confound your way. And vpon euery one,
That therein walketh, will deſtruétion fall.
Euen then ; when leaſt (perhaps) you thinke theron.

   Though, in the world ; you long haue had the names
Of honourable, honeſt, iuſt, and wiſe :

                        Walkt

Walkt in a courſe approu'd, and left your fames
To after ages ; in large Hiſtories.
 Though you are great ; and Orators can hire ;
To cloke your foule proceedings, with faire ſhowes ;
Or, to defame the Righteous, here conſpire.
And make abhorr'd, the path in which he goes.
 Though, at your deaths, with formall pietie,
And workes of publike loue, you often do
Conceale, your rotten hearts hypocriſie :
Deceiuing ſo, your ſelues, and others to.
 And, at your funerals, haue preacht abrod ;
A glorious rumor, of a bleſſed end :
Thoſe clouds, can neuer blinde the ſight of God.
But ruine, ſhall your wicked courſe, attend.
 Though you ; the ancient Heathens *prais'd mora-*
The Iewiſh *ſtrictneſſe ; the hot Zealouſneſſe* *(lities ;*
Of Schiſmaticks *haue learn'd : with* Romes *forma-*
To trim your way, *with ſhewes of happineſſe.* *(lities,*
 And though, the Paſſenger *that walks it, carries*
A lode of pardons : mumbling, as he goes,
Fiue thouſand Creedes ; ten thouſand Ave Maries :
And, of his owne good merits, addes to thoſe.
 Yet, all will faile him ; yea, there's many a one,
By you, for Saints canoniz'd ; whom your path
        · Hath

Hath thither brought : where, now they lie & grone,
Beneath the burthen of Gods heauy wrath.

   For, he, *approues no meanes of happineffe,*
Or way of feruing him ; but that which he
Hath taught himfelfe : And, it is wickedneffe ;
Another courfe to feeke, what ere it be.

   This you haue done, you finners ; fo, for this :
Your way, and you, fhall perifh. And while thofe
Whofe courfe you haue derided ; dwell in bliffe ;
You ; all contentment, fhall for euer lofe.

   That (fince you would not vnderftand aright,
The path *that leads to fafety ; whilft you might)*
You fhould, when you are paft returning ; know,
It was the Way, *that you defpifed fo.*

* * * * * * * *

THus ; haue I fung the fum, of what the *Mufe*
  Of our great *Prophet* ; in this *Ode,* purfues.
The way to *Bliffe.* Which, as my weakneffe can,
I ftriue to leuell fo ; that euery man ;
Yea, little children, may come walke along :
And make it fhort, and eafie, with a *fong.*

              Here,

Here, warne I all ; but here, I cannot ſay
Enough, to perfect all men, in that *way.*
For, ſome lacke one thing ; ſome another miſſe,
To further on, their voiage vnto *bliſſe.* (ledge want.
Some, faith ; ſome, works ; ſome, loue ; ſome know-
In ſome, repentance ; in ſome, grace, is ſcant.
The greateſt part ; defectiue finde, I ſhall,
Of moſt of theſe ; and many men of all.
Then, ſome diſpaire ; and ſome preſume as far.
Some, too ſecure ; and ſome, too penſiue are.
Some, pray not ; and ſome, praiſe not God aright.
That each man therfore ; he, well furniſh might,
For this aduenture ; and with meanes diuine,
Aſſiſt him, from his heauenly *Magazine.*
To fit their ſeuerall wants ; he offers you
A hundred nine and forty (in a row)
Of ſuch Inſtructions : as, who e're ſhall pleaſe,
To weigh their vſe, and liue, and walke, by theſe.
My life for theirs ; at length, they ſhall attaine
That happineſſe, their ſoules, deſires to gaine.
And to aſſiſt their weake ſimplicities,
That cannot ſute, their owne neceſſities,
In that rich treaſurye.   My humble *Muſe*
Shall be their Guide ; their Seruant ; and refuſe

                                                    No

No paines (if Gods great Prouidence permit)
Till all thefe facred *Oracles*, fhe fit
To their capacities. So, I fhall be
A help to them : And they may further me,
By their good prayers, in that bleffed path :
Whofe end, contentment, euerlafting hath.

THE

THE
PARAPHRASE;
WHERIN THE WORDS

of the Pſalme, are wholy retai-
ned : and diſtinguiſhed from
the reſt by a change of
LETTER.

BLeſſed is the man, that, being in
the firſt eſtate of innocency
doth not walke from it, after the
euill affections of corrupted nature :
in the lewd *Counſels of the vngodlie*;
By conſenting vnto euill concupi-
ſcences, *Nor ſtand in the* broad *way
of ſinners*, acting, and perſeuering in
euill : *Nor ſit, in the* infectious *ſeat of
the ſcornfull* ; ſcoffing vertue, deri-
ding religion ; or, by falſe doctrines
(and

Verſe 1.

(and euill examples) peruerting o-
thers.

Verse 2.

For, hee is such an one; who, is
not carefull onely, to auoyd euill.
But, is enclined to good also. *His de-
light is* seriously *in the Law of the*
L O R D. *And, in his* eternall *Law*
(that hee may know, teach, and ful-
fill it; in thought, word, and deed)
doth he meditate vpon all occasions;
and at all times; euen, *Day and night*,
without intermission.

Verse 3.

In this; consisteth the meanes of
his felicity. *And he shall be like a* flou-
rishing *Tree*; which, the Diuine Pro-
uidence hath *planted, by the riuers of
waters.* For, as such a Tree, being
nourished by those streames, hath
the meanes *that will* enable *it*, to *bring
forth his fruit in due season* : so, the
Blessed Man, being planted by the
fountaines of Grace, flowing from
the Holy Spirit of God ; bringeth
forth in due time, the fruits of faith,
and

and good workes, to eternall life.
And, in the greateft drought, recci-
ueth fuch refrefhing ; that *his leafe
fhall not fade.* A word of his, fhall
not be in vaine (though, for the pre-
fent, it feeme to fall to the ground)
but it fhall take effect. *And whatfo-
euer he doth fhall profper,* at laft ; both
to his euerlafting glory and the in-
ftruction of others.

Now, *the vngodly* ; becaufe, they
walke after their owne Counfels, *are
not fo* bleffed : neither, doth any
thing they take in hand, fo profper.
But, they, *are like the chaffe, which the
winde driueth away.* For, as that is
dry, vnfruitfull, and therfore carried
about with euery puffe ; fo, they
wanting the moyfture of grace, are
therfore ouer-light ; and the fpirit of
the Deuill, the winde of pride, temp-
tations, and euill affections : vnfet-
ledly hurrie them to and fro, without
reft.

Verfe 4.

M   And,

175

Verſe 5. And, by reaſon of this ; euen be-
cauſe, theſe vanities carry them from
God. *Therfore, the vngodly ſhall not*
be able to *ſtand*, as innocent, before
him, *in the Iudgement.* Whether it
be that, which he ſhall be pleaſed to
inflict on them, in this life : or, at the
laſt Day. *Nor*, ſhall falſe worſhip-
pers, or ſuch *Sinners* ; who haue neg-
lected this meanes of Bleſſedneſſe :
be admitted *in the Congregation of the
Righteous*, among thoſe, to whom
God (hauing ſeparated them at his
right hand) ſhall hereafter ſay :
Come, yee bleſſed of my Father,
&c.

Verſe 6. And all this, commeth thus to
paſſe. *For* that, *the* L O R D accep-
teth, *knoweth*, and alloweth, *the* vn-
defiled *way of the Righteous*, and the
courſes, which they follow, to attaine
this bleſſedneſſe. *But*, contrariwiſe,
ſo abhorreth *the way of the vngodly* ;
that the endeauors, of thoſe Repro-
bates,

bates, *ſhall periſh,* with them, in eternall damnation.

The Prayer:

Wherin, the ſcope of this Pſalme is conſidered: and the bleſſedneſſe there mentioned, implored of God.

OH thou eternall Son, of the euer-liuing God. Who, art the way of life, the meanes of all true *Bleſſedneſſe,* and the onely Happy One; who, continuing in thy integrity, haſt both auoyded, all manner of ſinne; and euery way fulfilled the whole Law, and will of thy Father. Thou, oh Chriſt; who art that *tree of life,* which brought forth the fruit of our ſaluation, in *due ſeaſon:* and without whom, none can

euer haue fure hope, to become hap-
py. Grant, oh fweet Redeemer ; that
by the imputation of thy righteouf-
neffe ; we, who are fallen from our
firft Integrity, may bee regenerated,
and made fpotleffe againe, in thy
fight. Sanctifie our polluted hearts,
that they may no more wander after,
the vaine *counfels*, of *vngodly* affecti-
ons. Let them not haue power, to
allure vs into the *way* of finfull acti-
ons. Or, if we doe (through frailty)
at any time, ftray from Thee, into
the trodden path of *Sinners*, which
leadeth to deftruction (as wee muft
acknowledge, we often doe.)   Bring
vs backe, oh fweet *Iefu* ; and let vs
not *ftand* there, vntill we lofe the fee-
ling of our finnes : and forget for e-
uer to returne ; but, let euery flip be
attended,   with   immediate   repen-
tance, to whip vs vp againe ; left the
iteration of finne, bring vs at length,
to the *feat of fcorners*, and the deniall
of

of Thee. Keepe vs; oh keepe vs, from that low ebb of grace; yea, although we often run far into the *way of ſinners*; and many times carelefly *ſtand* ſtill, when thou calleſt vs from thence : yet, of all mercies, wee entreat thee, that we neuer bee ſuffered to ſtray ſo wide, from the way of *Bleſſedneſſe*: to ſin againſt thy Holy Spirit. Or, to *ſit* downe in that *ſeat* of *peſtilence*, which may infect our ſoules, to eternall death.

And, to enable vs the better, to ſhun ſuch dangers; we befeech thee, poſſeſſe our hearts with thy loue; and a true delight in thy Word. Let thy *Law*, *day and night*, openly and ſecretly, in aduerſity and proſperity, bee our principall ſtudy, and practiſe, all the time of our life. Faſhion vs, to thine own Image; let thy right hand *plant* vs, in thine owne Vineyard.

And, that we may bee, as fruitfull-flouriſhing *Trees*, bringing forth fea-

M 3 fonable

fonable fruits, to thy glory, and the profit of thy *Church*. Let the plenti-full *Riuers* of thy Grace, water vs; vntill we grow vp, and become fit to bee replanted, in thy eternall *Para-dife*. Let our words, as the *leaues* of a fruitfull tree ; be a continuall orna-ment vnto vs: feruing alfo, to heale the wounded confciences of our weake brethren. And although, for a time, thou fuffereft vs, to appeare miferable and vnhappy ; yet, let all things (euen the afflictions which we haue had) *profper* vs in the way, to e-uerlafting *Bleffeneffe*.

And, forafmuch, as thofe, who de-light not in thy feruice, are in a mife-rable condition ; and nothing fo hap-py, as thy children, whatfoeuer they feem to the world. Grant, ô Lord, that wee (being warned by thy difplea-fure againft them) may truly worfhip thee, & haue euer fuch a meafure of faith, and of thy grace ; as may keep

vs

vs ſetled in our conſciences, & quiet, from the fury of thoſe affections, that carry them headlong into end-leſſe vnreſt. And when thou ſhalt caſt that *chaffe*, into the fire ; purge vs, thy ſeruants, from corruption ; and lay vs up, as pure wheat, in thy Heauenly Granard.

Heare vs, oh deere Redeemer ; and when that dreadfull day com-meth, wherein thou ſhalt ſummon the whole world to *Iudgement.* Let vs not, be thruſt among thoſe guil-ty ones, who ſhall fall, and bee con-founded with horrour, at thy pre-ſence. But make vs able to *ſtand*, in that fearfull doome ; place vs at thy right hand, in that righteous Congre-gation, into which, no vnrepentant *ſinners* ſhall be admitted. And, when thou ſhalt turne them off, with that terrible anſwer ; *I know you not.* Let vs ; oh let vs, bee receiued into thy mercy. And ſeeing, wee ſeeke for

M 4 *Bleſſed-*

Bleſſedneſſe, by that way and meanes
onely, which thou haſt appoynted :
Acknowledge it, as thine owne or-
dinance ; and, though we are a while
the ſcorne of the world, make vs at
·length, Inheritors of that vnſpeaka-
ble felicity, which wee ſhall enioy in
Thee.   So, both in our ſafeties, and
in the deſtruction of thine ene-
mies alfo ; ſhall thy name
be glorified, now and
for euer. *Amen.*

(***)

To

To fill vp the vacant pages of this ſheet, here is added, as neceſſary, to ſtir the Reader vp to theſe ſtudies; a metricall Paraphraſe, vpon the firſt eight verſes, of the 12 Chapter of *Eccleſiaſtes,* beginning thus:

Remember thy Creatour, in the dayes of thy youth, &c.

N*Ow* Young-man; *thy Creator thinke vpon;*
   Before the prime, of luſty Youth *be gone.*
Now; e're at hand, that euill day appeares;
With thoſe vnwelcome and abhorred yeares:
When thou (deiected) ſhalt, the world contemne,
And grecued ſay; I haue no ioy in them.   *(retaine,*
   Now; whilſt Sun, Moone, *and* Stars, *their light*
And no black clouds, *doe threat a ſecond* raine.
Before, the Keepers of the houſe *doe ſhrinke.*
Before, with trembling knees, the Strong men *ſinke.*
Before, the Grinders *leſs'ned, quiet lye;*   *prye.*
And they *grow* darke, *that through the* windowes
                                              Before

Before, the Doores without, *faſt cloſed bin,*
Through their baſe ſound, that faintly grinde *within.*
Before, the Bird *to riſe, doth ſummon thee* ;
And Muſiques Daughters *quite abaſed bee.*
Before, the lofty thing *doe this diſmay* ;
And ſhuddring ſcare *ſurprize thee in the* way.
Before the Almond *put his flowers abrode,*
The Graſhopper, *become a heauy lode,*
Deſires *decay, and lothed* Age *thou meet* ;
Or troops of Mourners, *waiting in the ſtreet.*
   Oh, doe not thou the time, till then prolong.
But minde him, whilſt the ſiluer Cord *is ſtrong.*
Now ; *whilſt the* Golden Ewre, *vncras'd is found* :
And at the Fountaine-head *the* Pitcher *ſound.*
Before the Wheele, *be at the* Cyſterne *tore,*
Or Duſt *grow earth, as earth it was before* :
And, from the bodies quite diſſolued frame ;
The ſoule returne to God, from whence it came.
   Thus ſpake the Preacher.   And he told vs why :
   For all (ſayd he) is vaineſt vanity.

                                                      The|

The fame, another way paraphrafed, accor-
ding to the fignification of the feuerall
Metaphors.

(heat,

N*Ow; whilft warme bloud, with frefh & kindly*
Doth through each part, with liuely vigor beat:
And all thy beauties, in their fpring-tide bee;
Thinke on thy God, that fo created thee.
Accept this fit aduantage of the time.
Giue him, the Firft-lings of thy golden prime.
Before, thy laft vnwelcome dayes, begin
To bring thofe yeeres, thou haft no pleafure in.
Now; while thou feeft profperities bright Sun,
Enlightens thee the way thou haft to run:
And Gods pure Word *affords a cheerfull light,*
To guide thee fafely, through blacke errors night.
Doe not forget, that thou a Maker *haft,*
Till all the morning of thy life be paft.
Nor wafte the time (from ftormes & troubles cleare)
Till greefes on greefes; like clouds on clouds appeare.
Thofe hands, *that youth a while doth powerfull*
Vnfteddy (through their feeblenes) fhall fhake.(make;

Thofe

Those legs, *that strongly doe vphold thee, now* ;
With aches pained, shall beneath thee bow.
Thy few loose teeth, *will cease their food to grinde* ;
And thy dim eyes, *stand in their cazements blinde.*
Thy iawes, *their nimble motion quite shall lose.*
Thy lips *sunke in, their double wickers close.*
Thy wonted sleepe, *thy temples shall forgoe* ;
And daily raise thee, when the Cocke *doth crow.*
Thy listning eares, *their sense aside shall lay :*
And euery rub, *disturb thee in the way.*
The siluer haires, *thou on thy head shalt haue :*
Will shew thee ready ripened for the graue.
Each trifling thing, *shall be a burthen to thee.*
The vaine desires *of youth, shall all forgoe thee.*
Thee ; *to his house, shall* Age *with panting breath*
Conduct ; *there lodge thee, in the bed of death,*
And those, who thither, thy attendants were,
Shall mourning, *home returne* ; *and leaue thee there.*
   Oh thou ! that wouldst a needfull comfort finde,
In those blacke dayes ; *now thy* Creator *minde.*
Before thy nerues *their sinewie vigor lacke :*
And strength, and marrow, *leaue thy weakned back,*
While neither cares, nor sorrowes, craze thy braine :
Whilst thy sound liuer, *fills vp every vaine.*

Whilst

Whilſt thou art yet in health ; *and feel'ſt thy* head,
By no heart-breaking pang diſtempered.
Ere fleſh *diſſolue to earth* ; *and* ſpirit *bee*
Return'd to Him, *that firſt did giue it thee.*
For then ; *this ſaying will moſt true appeare :*
That all is vaine, and nought but vaineſſe here.

Glory be to God.   Amen.

Correct thefe faults with thy pen.

PAg. 8. lin. 15. for *feemes*, read *feeme*. pag. 14. lin. 7. for *Catali-
ſticall*, in fome coppies, read *Cabaliſticall*. pag. 119. lin. the
laſt, for *whith*, read *with*. pag. 121. lin. 9. for *Righteoufneſſe*, in
fome coppies, read *Vnrighteoufneſſe*, pag. 124. lin. 23. for *thirſt*,
read *thrift*.

The Authours *Preparation to the Pfalter*, fom-
time mentioned in this Booke, is to bee fold at
the figne of the golden Vnicorne, in *Pater Noſter*
Row, by *Iohn Harrifon*.